T0257118

SVG Text Layout
Words as Art

Amelia Bellamy-Royds
& Kurt Cagle

Beijing · Boston · Farnham · Sebastopol · Tokyo

SVG Text Layout

by Amelia Bellamy-Royds and Kurt Cagle

Printed in the United States of America.

Published by O'Reilly Media, Inc., 1005 Gravenstein Highway North, Sebastopol, CA 95472.

O'Reilly books may be purchased for educational, business, or sales promotional use. Online editions are also available for most titles (*http://safaribooksonline.com*). For more information, contact our corporate/institutional sales department: 800-998-9938 or *corporate@oreilly.com*.

Editor: Meg Foley
Production Editor: Colleen Lobner
Copyeditor: Jasmine Kwityn
Proofreader: James Fraleigh

Indexer: Amelia Bellamy-Royds
Interior Designer: David Futato
Cover Designer: Ellie Volckhausen
Illustrator: Rebecca Demarest

November 2015:   First Edition

Revision History for the First Edition
2015-10-20:   First Release

See *http://oreilly.com/catalog/errata.csp?isbn=9781491933824* for release details.

978-1-491-93382-4

[LSI]

Table of Contents

Preface

Scalable Vector Graphics (SVG) consist of a markup language and associated style rules for defining images and diagrams. SVG is an image format, and for most people, text isn't the first thing they think of when considering the uses of SVG. From the beginning, however, a key feature of SVG has been its ability to encode text in a machine-readable form. Because SVG itself is a text-based markup language, the text characters in an SVG file can be viewed and edited in any text editor.

This book takes a deep dive into the use of text within SVG. It explores the creative possibilities, but also the potential pitfalls. It describes the basics, but also shows how you can use SVG to generate complex layouts. And, unfortunately, it also outlines the many inconsistencies and limitations of web browser implementations of SVG text (as of mid-2015, when this book was written).

This book was born from another project, an introduction to using SVG on the Web. In order to keep that book a manageable length—and keep it suitable for introductory audiences—many details and complexities had to be skimmed over. But those details and complexities add up to the full, wonderful potential of SVG as a graphics format. Once you understand the basics of SVG, you can start thinking about creating more intricate designs and more creative effects.

What We'll Cover

If you're reading this, hopefully you are already familiar with the basics of SVG: how to define a graphic as a set of shapes, and how to use that graphic either as a standalone image file or as markup in an

HTML page. It will also help if you are familiar with the basics of CSS-styled HTML text, as SVG text builds upon the basic CSS style rules.

The book starts with a brief overview of how computers display text content, and then steadily introduces the many ways SVG allows you to control the appearance of text:

- Chapter 1 reviews the basics of laying out text in word processors and websites, and introduces much of the technical terminology used to describe text.

- Chapter 2 introduces the SVG <text> element and the basic attributes for positioning simple text labels within a graphic, including the particular issues of sizing text within a scalable coordinate system.

- Chapter 3 briefly covers SVG's fill and stroke properties for controlling the visual appearance of text.

- Chapter 4 gets into more complex text layouts, using formatted poetry as examples.

- Chapter 5 explores SVG's ability to control the position and orientation of individual text characters.

- Chapter 6 introduces the text-anchor property and discusses how it affects the alignment of text.

- Chapter 7 considers the particular issues of multidirectional text, including right-to-left horizontal text and vertical text.

- Chapter 8 introduces the properties that control the vertical alignment of horizontal text and the horizontal alignment of vertical text.

- Chapter 9 looks at the <textPath> element and how it can be used to create curved or complex text layouts.

- Chapter 10 explores fonts and their impact on SVG text, including the use of the @font-face rule to incorporate web fonts in your SVG graphics online.

- Chapter 11 looks at the textLength attribute and font-size-adjust property, which can be used to standardize text layout when you don't have full control over the fonts used; the chapter also describes decorative uses for textLength.

- Finally, Chapter 12 introduces the SVG `<foreignObject>` element, and shows how it can be used to include CSS-formatted HTML text within an SVG image.

To complete the book, Appendix A provides a quick reference of the SVG text elements and their attributes, while Appendix B summarizes the related style properties.

About This Book

Whether you're casually flipping through the book, or reading it meticulously from cover to cover, you can get more from it by understanding the following little extras used to provide additional information.

Conventions Used in This Book

The following typographical conventions are used in this book:

Italic
> Indicates new terms, URLs, email addresses, filenames, and file extensions.

`Constant width`
> Used for program listings, as well as within paragraphs to refer to program elements such as variable or function names, databases, data types, environment variables, statements, and keywords.

`Constant width bold`
> Shows commands or other text that should be typed literally by the user.

`Constant width italic`
> Shows text that should be replaced with user-supplied values or by values determined by context.

> Tips like this will be used to highlight particularly tricky aspects of SVG, or simple shortcuts that might not be obvious at first glance.

Notes like this will be used for more general asides and interesting background information.

Warnings like this will highlight compatibility problems between different web browsers (or other software), or between SVG as an XML file versus SVG in HTML pages.

In addition, sidebars like the following will introduce supplemental information:

A Brief Aside

"Future Focus" sidebars will look at proposed features that aren't yet standardized, or new standards that aren't widely implemented.

Although these sidebars are not absolutely essential for understanding SVG colors, patterns, and gradients, they will hopefully add important context when planning a complete web project.

Using Code Examples

Supplemental material (code examples and figures) is available for download as a zip archive or Git repository:

https://github.com/oreillymedia/SVG_Text_Layout

Alternatively, you can view the examples online in your web browser:

http://oreillymedia.github.io/SVG_Text_Layout

The examples in this book have been tested in common web browsers in mid-2015. Bugs and inconsistencies are noted throughout. Hopefully, some of those bugs will be fixed in the future; web browsers are updated on a monthly basis, and some improvements have occured even as this book was being edited. However, there are likely other problems that we have overlooked. In addition, other software for manipulating SVG have their own limitations or quirks which are not outlined here. Test early, test often, test in any software your content needs to be displayed with.

This book is here to help you get your job done. In general, if example code is offered with this book, you may use it in your programs and documentation. You do not need to contact us for permission unless you're reproducing a significant portion of the code. For example, writing a program that uses several chunks of code from this book does not require permission. Selling or distributing a CD-ROM of examples from O'Reilly books does require permission. Answering a question by citing this book and quoting example code does not require permission. Incorporating a significant amount of example code from this book into your product's documentation does require permission.

We appreciate, but do not require, attribution. An attribution usually includes the title, author, publisher, and ISBN. For example: "*SVG Text Layout* by Amelia Bellamy-Royds and Kurt Cagle (O'Reilly). Copyright 2016 Amelia Bellamy-Royds, Kurt Cagle, 978-1-4919-3382-4."

If you feel your use of code examples falls outside fair use or the permission given above, feel free to contact us at *permissions@oreilly.com*.

Safari® Books Online

Safari Books Online is an on-demand digital library that delivers expert content in both book and video form from the world's leading authors in technology and business.

Technology professionals, software developers, web designers, and business and creative professionals use Safari Books Online as their primary resource for research, problem solving, learning, and certification training.

Safari Books Online offers a range of plans and pricing for enterprise, government, education, and individuals.

Members have access to thousands of books, training videos, and prepublication manuscripts in one fully searchable database from publishers like O'Reilly Media, Prentice Hall Professional, Addison-

Wesley Professional, Microsoft Press, Sams, Que, Peachpit Press, Focal Press, Cisco Press, John Wiley & Sons, Syngress, Morgan Kaufmann, IBM Redbooks, Packt, Adobe Press, FT Press, Apress, Manning, New Riders, McGraw-Hill, Jones & Bartlett, Course Technology, and hundreds more. For more information about Safari Books Online, please visit us online.

How to Contact Us

Please address comments and questions concerning this book to the publisher:

O'Reilly Media, Inc.
1005 Gravenstein Highway North
Sebastopol, CA 95472
800-998-9938 (in the United States or Canada)
707-829-0515 (international or local)
707-829-0104 (fax)

We have a web page for this book, where we list errata, examples, and any additional information. You can access this page at *http://bit.ly/svg-text-layout*.

To comment or ask technical questions about this book, send email to *bookquestions@oreilly.com*.

For more information about our books, courses, conferences, and news, see our website at *http://www.oreilly.com*.

Find us on Facebook: *http://facebook.com/oreilly*

Follow us on Twitter: *http://twitter.com/oreillymedia*

Watch us on YouTube: *http://www.youtube.com/oreillymedia*

Acknowledgments

Parts of this book can trace their lineage through various manuscripts adapted and revised over multiple years. The list of people to thank for getting it finally to publication is therefore likewise long. Meg Foley is the editor of record, and deserves great appreciation for her unwavering cheerfulness in the face of stretched deadlines. Before her, Meghan Blanchette and Simon St.Laurent persevered through the unenviable task of herding authors of a technical manuscript in an ever-updating field.

The final book owes much to the team of technical reviewers— David Eisenberg, Robert Longson, Dudley Storey, and Tavmjong Bah—who identified errors and inconsistencies, suggested new figures and examples, and pointed out changing SVG implementations worth noting in the tips and warnings. As always, any lingering mistakes are entirely the responsibility of the imperfect authors. Taking care of a different type of technical issue, production editor Colleen Lobner and the rest of O'Reilly's production team helped finesse the book into a professional final form. Among them, special appreciation goes to copyeditor Jasmine Kwityn for her uncanny ability to detect inconsistencies in style and terminology, even from one chapter to another.

Finally, sincere thanks go out to all the developers working with SVG, creating software to implement it, or extending and improving the SVG specifications. Many of the tips and warnings collected in this book were derived from the experiences of others, shared through blogs, mailing lists, and more.

CHAPTER 1

Understanding Text Layout

The history of human writing includes etchings in stone and wood, impressions in clay tablets, ink applied with brushes, and ink applied with quill pens. The different means of writing have each influenced the visual appearance of the text that results.

As the technology used to create writing changed, first with the printing press, then the typewriter, then computer displays, so has the written form. In addition, geopolitical history has had its influence on writing, spreading scripts from one part of the world to another, where the writing system is adapted to different spoken languages.

This chapter reviews the core concepts common to text layout in all web documents. It starts with an introduction to the terminology used to describe letters and writing systems. It then looks at how text content, fonts, and text-rendering software combine to create text on computer displays. In particular, we focus on how markup languages like HTML, XML, and SVG interact with styling rules in CSS to define text layout within web browsers. Finally, we review the main features of SVG text layout, as a big-picture introduction to the rest of the book.

The Language of Text

When describing written text, there are some important distinctions to make between the concepts of written language and its execution in physical form. If you are going to make sense of a book about

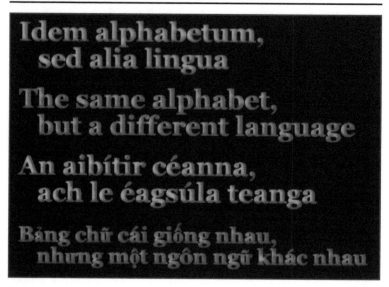

Figure 1-1. A phrase translated into many languages—from top to bottom: Latin, English, Irish Gaelic, and Vietnamese

text, you need to understand the words we use to describe the words we write.

Text is a physical embodiment of language. A *language* is a system of verbal or written communication whose practitioners can mostly understand one another. Written languages can be classified according to the script (or scripts) used to display them; for example, all the languages in Figure 1-1 use the Latin alphabet.

A *script* is a writing system used by one or more languages. The written symbols used in a script may be phonetic, where each symbol represents a sound. This includes alphabets, where symbols represent distinct consonant and/or vowel sounds, and also syllabaries, where symbols represent entire syllables. Other scripts are ideographic, where each symbol represents an entire word or concept.

The Latin script used to write English is also used by most Western European languages, among others. Someone fluent in English would recognize the letters used to write Gaelic or Vietnamese, even if the meaning of the text was impenetrable. Nonetheless, the division between scripts and languages is not always clear-cut; the complete modern Latin script used in those languages—and French,

German, Finnish, and many more—includes special characters and accents rarely used in English.

Some languages are written in multiple scripts, as alternatives or in combination. For example, Japanese is written with four different scripts:

- Kanji (ideographic characters similar to those used in Chinese and Korean)
- Hiragana (phonetic characters used to indicate words by their pronunciation or to express grammatical variations of kanji ideographs)
- Katakana (a distinct but related set of phonetic characters, mostly used for words of foreign origin and technical terms)
- Rōmaji (phonetic spelling using Latin—or Roman—letters, used for inputting text to computers or for some words adopted from European languages)

Most Japanese documents use kanji ideographs combined with kana (hiragana and katakana) syllables; Latin characters, however, are often integrated for special symbols, as demonstrated in the hand-written fishmarket sign shown in Figure 1-2.

Some characters, such as numeric digits and punctuation, are used in multiple scripts. On the other hand, some Latin letters look quite similar to letters in Greek or Cyrillic scripts, but they are not directly interchangeable, and may be associated with quite different sounds.

The *character* is the basic unit within the script. Phonetic letters are characters, ideographs are characters, but so are digits, punctuation marks, and the funny little faces called emoticons or emoji.

A character is a conceptual representation, independent of its specific presentation on screen or paper. In contrast, a *glyph* is the visual representation of the letter, digit, or symbol in a particular writing style. If you think of the other meaning of the word character—characters in a story or play—the glyph would be the actor who brings that character to life.

Glyphs can vary quite significantly depending on the way the text is formed: imagine what the paragraph you're reading would look like written in a school child's pencil, a calligrapher's fountain pen, or a medieval monk's Gothic brush strokes. Or if your imagination is not

Figure 1-2. A sign advertising horn snails for sale at a Tokyo fishmarket using a mix of kanji and kana characters, as well as latinized Arabic numerals and a Latin "g" as the symbol for grams (photograph by Wikimedia Commons contributor jibun)

that powerful, consider Figure 1-3, which uses computer fonts to create the same contrast. The shapes of the glyphs are very different from one line of text to the next, but the meaning of the characters is the same.

Even within a given writing system and style, the correct glyph for a character sometimes depends on the language used, adjacent characters, or the position within a word, so there can be multiple glyphs per character. In other cases, multiple characters are represented by the same glyph, such as the minus sign and the hyphen. Some characters are drawn by combining multiple glyphs (e.g., accented letters), while some sequences of characters are replaced by a combined glyph (known as a *ligature*). In some cases, ligature substitutions are a standard feature of how the language is written, required for effective communication. In other cases, these are optional stylistic effects.

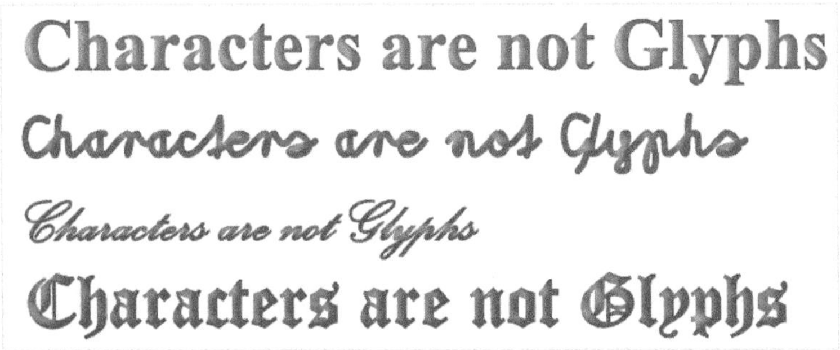

Characters are not Glyphs

Figure 1-3. *Four ways of writing "Characters are not Glyphs," with different styles of glyphs—from top to bottom: Times New Roman as implemented by Monotype for Microsoft, Morado Felt by Peter Wiegel, Palace Script MT, and Old English Text MT, both by Monotype*

A *typeface* or *font-face* is a specific collection of glyphs that have a consistent appearance. Many fonts only provide glyphs for characters in a specific script, but some try to provide a consistent appearance—as much as possible—across many different scripts. Nonetheless, many typographic traditions rely on inconsistencies in glyph appearance to express the structure of a complex text document, by distinguishing different sequences of text. A *font family* is a set of related typefaces that differ in certain stylistic features but have a harmonious appearance such that they could be used effectively together.

The faces within a family may vary according to their weight (boldness), style (e.g., italics), spacing and proportions, or other features. Figure 1-4 uses four different font families for Thai text to demonstrate how the overall appearance and proportions of the family are preserved between faces with different styles and weights.

In traditional typography—that is, typography based on arranging metal type in a printing press—a *font* consists of a specific typeface at a specific size. Most modern digital fonts, however, use vector graphics to define a scalable shape. A single font file can be adapted to any size (although many look better at larger sizes and a few are better when small) so the file is technically a font-face file. However, it is still useful to distinguish between the typeface as a design and the font file as an implementation in a particular file format.

Figure 1-4. Regular, italic, bold, and bold italic typefaces in four different font families—from top to bottom: Angsana New, JasmineUPC, IrisUPC, and LilyUPC; all fonts by Unity Progress Company

 Although most font formats only describe a single typeface per file, a few formats can define multiple faces of a font family within a single file.

Converting characters to glyphs is only the first step in text layout. Glyphs must be arranged on a page in a particular logical order to convey information. Greek, Latin, and Cyrillic scripts arrange characters in horizontal lines, left to right, as do many Indic scripts.

Other scripts are written right to left, particularly Middle Eastern scripts such as Arabic and Hebrew. A few languages (primarily the Asian ideographic scripts) are written top to bottom in traditional or formal documents. Each script and language has standards for how sequences of text—which may or may not be grouped into distinct words—and associated punctuation should be arranged into lines for optimal readability.

Text Layout on the Web

Regardless of how a writing system evolved—from chiseled marble or delicate brush strokes—rendering it on a computer display involves three sources of data interacting:

- The character data, defining the text to be displayed and maybe additional details about the language used, the significance of certain sections of text, and how they should be styled
- The font data, defining the glyphs to use for each character and maybe additional details on how to adjust the shape for better spacing, clearer rendering at low resolution, or ligature substitutions
- The text layout software's rules for selecting and arranging font glyphs to match given character data, including interpreting text in different scripts and languages, how to rearrange characters from different scripts, how to identify word breaks, how to space words on a page, and many more possibilities depending on the complexity of the software

For web documents, the character data is contained in the document markup or inserted into the document object model (DOM) by a script. The font data may be accessed from the user's operating system or downloaded as a supplementary resource; CSS style rules indicate which fonts should be used. The web browser (possibly aided by operating system software) is responsible for putting it all together, taking cues from the markup structure and the style rules provided by the web page author.

Character Data

Character data is a description of text in a form that the software may manipulate. The data may be derived from the user's keystrokes, retrieved from a file, received from a web server, or generated by a software algorithm.

Character data can even be created by character-recognition software from an image of written text or the user's movement on a tablet. However, without that interpretive step—translating the shapes of glyphs into corresponding characters—an image of text is not character data. Software cannot rearrange the text, display it in a different font, or read it aloud through a screen reader unless it can match that visual appearance to a standard representation of the character data in digital form.

Digital representations of text (i.e., computer files) use an *encoding* scheme to represent characters with binary data. Originally, there were separate encodings for each script, but in the late 1990s, *Unicode* started to change that. Unicode aims to describe all scripts in use—and many archaic ones—with a consistent encoding scheme. It's not there yet, and new characters are added every year, but it is a vast improvement over the days of incompatible encoding systems for every language.

Unicode, however, isn't a single character encoding; it is many. Unicode assigns a unique numerical *code point* to each character, but allows for multiple ways of representing that code point in binary data. Currently, the most common Unicode encodings vary according to how large a block of binary data is by default allocated to store the code point for each character: UTF-8 uses 8 bits (1 byte) per block, UTF-16 uses 16 bits (2 bytes).[1]

Characters that require more than one block start with flags that indicate how many blocks of data must be combined to get the correct encoding. In this way, any Unicode character can be represented in a UTF-8 file.

---

1 This is a vastly oversimplified discussion of character encodings in general and Unicode in particular. Joel Spolsky's 2003 article "The Absolute Minimum Every Software Developer Absolutely, Positively Must Know About Unicode and Character Sets (No Excuses!)" (*http://www.joelonsoftware.com/articles/Unicode.html*) should help fill you in on the rest.

Character encodings are usually hidden from the user in file meta-data or operating system settings. On the Web, however, where information is transmitted between computers with different operating systems and default languages, encodings must always be clearly defined. The HyperText Transfer Protocol (HTTP), used to pass web documents from servers to browsers, allows character encoding to be declared as part of the file's content type. Although this is the preferred approach, most document formats used on the Web also allow you to declare an encoding in the file itself.

In HTML and XML markup files, the character encoding can be declared using markup tags at the top of the file. This is possible because most character encodings use the same binary representation for the basic characters used in the markup syntax.

In HTML 5, the encoding is indicated with a `<meta>` element that has a `charset` attribute, like the following:

```
<html>
    <head>
        <meta charset="UTF-8" />
```

In older versions of HTML, the `http-equiv` meta element was used to substitute for the HTTP header declaring the character set:

```
<meta http-equiv="Content-Type"
      content="text/html; charset=UTF-8">
```

Whichever format is used, the declaration should appear as early as possible in the file.

In XML documents, including standalone SVG documents, character encoding is indicated at the very start of the text markup, with a processing instruction such as the following:

```
<?xml version="1.0" encoding='UTF-8'?>
```

If the XML declaration is included, the version number is mandatory, and should usually be `"1.0"` for SVG. XML version 1.1 has greater support for non-Latin characters in element `id` attributes and tag names, but these may not be supported in many SVG viewers.

For XML (and therefore SVG), browsers should be able to distinguish between UTF-8 and UTF-16 automatically. For graphical SVG, UTF-8 is usually preferred, as it efficiently stores the characters used for the SVG markup itself. You don't need to declare UTF-8 encoding with a processing instruction, but you do need to ensure that your code editor (or other software) saves the file in UTF-8 format.

Many text editors, and even code editors, save files in the older ASCII or ANSI encodings by default. Depending on the software, you may be able to change the default in user preferences. In other software, you will need to specify the encoding every time you save. Avoid future headaches by learning how to set the encoding in the software you are using!

If you are including many multibyte characters (e.g., if the text consists of mostly ideographic scripts), UTF-16 may be more appropriate. Other encodings should be avoided now that Unicode is widely supported, but if they are used, they should always be declared using a processing instruction. You may also need to change your web server's setting to ensure that it is not declaring a conflicting encoding.

The official names for character encodings are registered with the Internet Assigned Numbers Authority (*http://www.iana.org/assignments/ character-sets/character-sets.xhtml*).

SVG, HTML, and XML are text-based markup languages, where the structure and features of the document are indicated within the character data. The angle brackets (less-than/greater-than signs, < and >) separate the markup from the plain-text content that will be displayed. Supplementary text may be included in quoted attributes within the markup tags.

In SVG, not all plain-text content of the document is displayed; some is used for metadata and alternative text descriptions of the graphics.

Because markup characters have special meaning when reading the file, they cannot be used to represent the actual character within the text content. The Standard Generalized Markup Language (from which HTML, XML, and SVG are derived) introduced character entities, which start with an ampersand (&) and end with a semicolon (;), to represent these special characters.

In XML in general and SVG in particular, there are only five defined entities:

- `&lt;` for the less-than sign, <
- `&gt;` for the greater-than sign, >
- `&amp;` for the ampersand, &
- `&apos;` for the apostrophe or single straight quote, '
- `&quot;` for the double straight quotation mark, "

The less-than sign and ampersand *must* be encoded within XML text content; the others are usually optional.

In HTML, there are dozens of defined entities to represent common characters that cannot be represented in all character encodings or typed with all keyboard layouts. Examples include `&hellip;` for … (horizontal ellipsis) or `&eacute;` for é (lowercase *e* with an acute accent).

HTML is also more lenient about bare ampersands in text content; if they are not followed by the rest of a valid character entitity, they will be treated as plain text.

 HTML entities may be used within SVG markup included inline in an HTML 5 document, but not in standalone SVG files.

In XML or HTML, characters that cannot be encoded directly or by a defined character entity can be represented using the Unicode code point. The numeric code point value can be expressed using either the decimal or hexadecimal notation for the number: for example, `&#8756;` and `&#x2234;` These numeric character entities both represent the mathematical "therefore" sign (∴), which can also be represented in HTML by `&there4;`.

To ensure the correct interpretation of your text, particularly by accessibility technologies, you should also declare the human language of the content. This is done with the `lang` attribute in HTML or the `xml:lang` attribute in XML and SVG. In both cases, the value of the attribute is a language code consistent with the Internet Engineering Task Force's "Tags for Identifying Languages"—currently, RFC 5646 (*http://tools.ietf.org/html/rfc5646*).

In most cases, a two-letter language tag is sufficient, such as en for English or de for German (*Deutsch*). In other cases, a precise description of the language includes subtags, which add a country code (e.g., pt-BR for Brazilian Portuguese) or a script type (e.g., zh-Hans for simplified Chinese characters).

In both HTML and SVG, the language attribute applies to the text content and other attributes of the current element, as well as all nested elements, unless a nested element has its own language declaration. For single-language documents, therefore, it only needs to be specified once on the root <html> or <svg> element.

Font Data

Characters, as we have made clear, are not glyphs. On their own, the characters encoded in an SVG or HTML file do not have any visual representation. To display that character data on a screen, or print it on a page, the computer needs to pair it with a font.

The word *font* originates from metal-working foundries that created the type used in early printing presses. The mechanization of the written word standardized the appearance of individual glyphs within each printed page, but it also prompted the development of contrasting type designs for different purposes. Each font was a collection of letters and symbols which could be arranged to create a continuous section of text; different fonts set text at different sizes or with different styles.

The earliest computer fonts were collections of bitmapped images for each character: a fixed-size grid of points which should either be colored or not. The program displaying the text lined up each image one after the other on the display in the same way that metal type was lined up in a printing press.

Just as with metal type, each bitmapped font corresponds to a single size of text. If you need a different size of text, you need an alternative set of glyph data. If you want to print it on a device that allows finer resolution of colored points, you again need alternative glyphs.

Vector fonts addressed this issue by using mathematical lines and curves (quadratic or cubic Bézier curves) to define the shapes of each glyph, regardless of how many points of color fit within that shape. Vector fonts were first used in printers, particularly with Adobe's PostScript typesetting tools. Apple and Microsoft collaborated (imagine!) to introduce vector fonts to computer interfaces with the TrueType font format.

Vector fonts, however, are limited by the resolution of the display in another way: the curves may be infinitely scalable, but computer monitors are not. Elegant shapes become distorted and illegible when forced to fit the pixel grid at small scales. Both PostScript and TrueType fonts include additional data or instructions (known as font *hints*) for adjusting the curves to fit the display grid at small sizes. Figure 1-5 shows how these hints modify the vector outlines to create results similar to the blocky shapes of a purely bitmapped version; at higher resolutions, a much more accurate representation of the outline is possible.

TrueType was widely successful, but designers already had their favorite PostScript fonts. The OpenType specification was developed to make it easier for PostScript fonts to be used with software designed for TrueType. It allowed either format of vector data to be packaged in a file with a consistent structure and metadata.

 The OpenType file structure was an extension of the TrueType format, and TrueType fonts are also valid OpenType fonts. As a result, True-Type/OpenType fonts have continued to use the *.ttf* file extension for backward compatibility. Old software might not use new OpenType features, but can still access the basic font data.

There have been many other font file formats, using various mathematical models to define the shapes of glyphs and various programming languages to describe how those glyphs should be adjusted in different uses. On the Web, however, the OpenType fonts are currently dominant. Newer font formats such as WOFF (Web Open Font Format) are variations on the OpenType structure, with improved data compression and added metadata information.

Basic digital fonts, whether bitmapped or vector, follow the model of metal type. Individual characters map to individual glyphs that can then be lined up in neat rows. By default, this can create an unpleas-

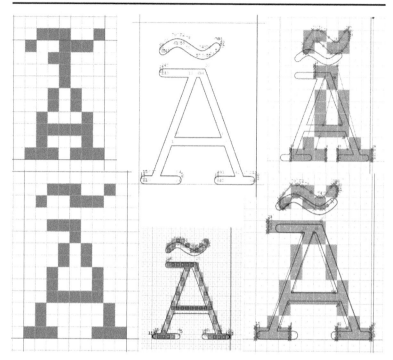

Figure 1-5. Vector and bitmapped font variations on the letter Ã in the Courier typeface: in Microsoft's bitmapped Courier font at 13px and 17px font size (left); as the TrueType vector outline for Monotype's Courier New font (center top); the Courier New outlines adjusted to fit to the same 13 and 17px font sizes (right); the same Courier New outline rasterized at higher resolution and with anti-aliasing (bottom center); composite of screenshots from FontForge font editing software

antly chunky appearance. Most font formats include *kerning* instructions to adjust the spacing between certain pairs of characters.

For many scripts, particularly those based more on handwriting than on printed type, kerning is not sufficient. Glyphs need to adjust not only in spacing, but also in shape or even position, according to the character sequence.

OpenType has introduced numerous features for defining optional and required substitutions of glyphs for given sequences of characters. However, not all fonts will include these options, and not all software will know how to use them. Other font formats incorporate more complex *text shaping* rules directly in the font data, but for OpenType much of the text shaping decisions must be made by the layout engine.

Even when all substitutions and rearrangements are made, the font data still consists of individual glyphs (although not only one glyph per character). The appearance of connected *cursive* text is created by overlapping the ending stroke of one glyph with the starting stroke of the next.

Text Layout Instructions

The printing-press typographer slid sequences of metal type on to alignment rails. Each letter took up just as much space as it needed, and the font came with a variety of spacers to place in between words, as necessary to adjust the lengths of each line for pleasing balance. The lines of text were then fit together with additional metal spacers to create a page.

 These spacers, made out of lead, are the source of the typographic term *leading* (pronounced *led-ing*) to describe spacing between lines of text.

Modern word processors—and related text-layout software such as the web browser—attempt to re-create that pleasing balance with the application of clear rule sets. The font data indicates how much space each glyph should consume in a line. The software may also use the font to insert ligatures or adjust kerning.

The layout software, however, is solely responsible for arranging the font glyphs into a logical document according to the standards of the script and language. Most text layout software uses rules to determine appropriate word breaks—for the language and script—at which to start a new line or insert extra space for a justified align-ment. (Rules for determining appropriate hyphenation breaks are more complex, and therefore less common.) Other language-sensitive rules may be used to transform the case of text or re-arrange the order of characters when scripts with different directions are mixed together.

Because the breaks and spacing are determined automatically, a word processor can adjust and reflow the lines of text if the content or styles are changed, removing and inserting line breaks as required. This is a key feature of web browser display of HTML text; it flows to fit the size of the display.

The automatically generated layout may not be quite as pleasing as text positioned by a skilled typographer, but it is much more flexible. On the Web, this is particularly important for web layouts that are responsive to devices with different sized screens. To display a photograph or other image on a smaller screen, it needs to be scaled down in all directions. Text, however, can wrap to fill more lines with the same size font.

Although web browsers are quite content to lay out plain HTML text according to default rules, Cascading Style Sheets (CSS) offer many ways to customize the output. Text styling instructions can be loosely classified into categories:

- Character manipulation properties, such as `text-transform`, `direction`, and `unicode-bidi`, define transformations to the character data that should be applied before converting characters into glyphs.

- Font properties, such as `font-weight`, `font-stretch`, or `font-variant`, determine which font file is used and what features of the font are activated.

- Text styling properties, such as `text-decoration` or `letter-spacing`, modify the appearance of continuous sequences of glyphs.

- Text layout properties, such as `text-justify`, `text-indent`, `line-height`, and `white-space`, control how rows of glyphs are divided and arranged into blocks of text.

- Page layout properties, such as `width`, `height`, `padding`, and `margin`, determine how blocks of text are positioned on the page, and indirectly set the maximum length of each text line.

This book assumes that you are at least moderately familiar with using CSS to style HTML text. The categories distinguished here are emphasized because they correspond to the areas where CSS-styled SVG text layout and CSS-styled HTML text layout overlap, and where they diverge.

Text Within Scalable Vector Graphics

SVG is a graphic language, used to define geometric shapes and graphical effects for rendering them. SVG images are often embedded within HTML text, and SVG markup may be included directly with HTML 5 files.

Text within SVG itself is often an afterthought. Nonetheless, words within graphics are indispensable as annotations for charts, presentations, and maps, assigning context to the size of a pie chart wedge or forming a label for a color in a legend. There is also a more artistic side of SVG text: words as *art*.

The phrase "word art" has a somewhat besmirched reputation, thanks to the ease by which colorful distorted words can be created in some office software—and the corresponding overuse by some office managers to decorate every office memo. But a tool is only as useful as the person wielding it, and it should not be discarded just because it has been misused.

Calligraphy—literally, beautiful writing—is even today considered an art form. The modern typographer is far more artist than technician, extending the art of beautiful, engaging, and sometimes horrific or amusing, writing into the electronic realm.

It is thus perhaps not surprising that SVG included a fairly rich library for handling text, both for laying out lines of text and for the creation of fonts and font glyphs (the graphics that describe each letter).

Unfortunately, SVG fonts were sufficiently different from the OpenType font formats used by web browsers that Firefox and Internet Explorer never implemented them. In particular, the SVG font specification did not include any equivalents to the more advanced OpenType glyph-selection features essential for the correct rendering of some scripts.

SVG fonts are still supported on WebKit and iOS devices, but the Chromium project has removed support for SVG fonts from Blink-based browsers. This book therefore focuses on the layout of text, and the selection and use of existing fonts.

It is important to realize that SVG uses nearly the same CSS properties for selecting and styling fonts that HTML does. This means in practice that if you know how to style text in HTML, you already know many of the ways to style text within SVG.

An equally important realization is that SVG uses a completely *different* model from CSS/HTML when it comes to positioning text on the screen. SVG text layout has as much in common with the layout of SVG shapes as it does with CSS layout of flowing text in an HTML page.

Text in SVG is drawn exactly where you position it, and does not reposition itself if it bumps into other text or overflows the edge of the image. If the graphic as a whole changes size, the text scales down with the imagery; it does not reflow.

SVG text layout is a hugely complex topic. At its most basic, it consists of an instruction to the browser to "write this text here." At its most complex, it allows you to carefully position individual letters in geometric patterns, with nearly as much control as you position your SVG shapes.

Nearly as much control, but not quite. Text positioning within SVG is always a balance between the designer who knows what is best for the graphic, and the software that knows (or should know) what is best for the particular font and linguistic scripts being used.

You can minimize the variability by trying to ensure that the browser will use the font you designed with, either by using a common system font or by making a web font available by reference. However, the use of these fonts is still not guaranteed. Careful design is required to ensure the layout is acceptable with alternative fonts. Additional properties and attributes are available to tell the browser how much space you expected the text to fill.

Unfortunately, text is one of the worst areas in SVG for cross-browser inconsistencies. Many of the more nuanced layout options defined in the specifications cannot be relied on for documents that will be distributed on the Web. As much as possible, this book warns you about the major incompatibilities at the time of writing (mid-2015). However, the best defense against unexpected results is to test in as many browsers and operating systems as you need to support.

This is particularly true when working outside Latin scripts. The SVG specifications introduced a number of features that were intended to offer support for all types of writing systems, including right-to-left and top-to-bottom scripts. The well-meaning but overly complicated internationalization options have never been well implemented, and are in the midst of being rewritten by new CSS specifications. Nonetheless, they are worth keeping in mind, whether you create multilingual documents or whether you would like to use vertical text for graphical effect. In the meantime, you can re-create many of these layouts using SVG's manual positioning options. Chapter 7 discusses both the standard features and the workarounds.

 A key feature of SVG text is that it can be filled and stroked like any SVG shape, including with gradients and patterns. This book does not go into detail about SVG's painting options, but it does highlight a few of the ways in which painting text is unique.

After working through this book, you will find that there are very few text layouts that you *can't* create with SVG. However, that does not mean it is always the best tool for the job.

The control that SVG text layout offers comes at the cost of the automatic line layout and reflowing text available with CSS-styled HTML. In many cases, it is much easier and more responsive to use HTML and CSS text layout. The SVG specifications even allow you to embed HTML within SVG (using the `<foreignObject>` element that we'll discuss in Chapter 12) but again, incomplete browser support has limited its use.

Future Focus
Anticipating New Features

The SVG specifications are under development, with an SVG 2 standard expected to be completed in early 2016, and additional modules focusing on particular features. New proposals will vastly increase the flexibility of text within SVG, introducing many of the features of CSS/HTML text layout—when the specifications are finalized and implementations are available, that is. "Future Focus" sidebars like this one will emphasize when some of the information described in the main text is likely to change in the future.

At the same time, new CSS modules are integrating many features previously only available in SVG. We'll also use these sidebars to highlight areas where matching features are likely to be introduced to CSS-styled HTML text.

CHAPTER 2

SVG Text Basics

For the simplest use cases, SVG text is straightforward. A short label can be added to a diagram with a single markup element and a pair of attributes.

SVG text, like SVG shapes, are positioned within a two-dimensional coordinate system. The coordinate system can be controlled by viewBox attributes and transform properties, but by default it starts in the top-left corner of the graphic. All points in the image are defined by their position relative to that origin point, along the horizontal x-axis and vertical y-axis.

The rest of the book will assume you are familiar with the SVG coordinate system. If any of that sounded confusing, you might have some background reading to do.

Letters on a Page

SVG text is, conveniently enough, drawn using the <text> element. Attributes on the <text> element define the position at which to start writing. The child text content of the element provides the words and letters to be written. It looks something like this:

```
<text x="10px" y="80%">SVG Text</text>
```

Put that code in a 400×80 SVG file, on top of a background rectangle, as in Example 2-1, and the result looks like Figure 2-1.

Example 2-1. Defining text within an SVG

```
<svg xmlns="http://www.w3.org/2000/svg"
    xml:lang="en"
    width="4in" height="0.8in" viewBox="0 0 400 80" >
    <title>Basic SVG Text</title>
    <rect width="100%" height="100%" fill="lightYellow" />
    <text x="10px" y="80%">SVG Text</text>
</svg>
```

SVG Text

Figure 2-1. Unstyled text in an SVG

Which…isn't particularly exciting. But it confirms that yes, we can display text within an SVG file.

The text is positioned on the page using the x and y attributes on each <text> element. As with the positioning attributes used for SVG's basic shapes (circles, ellipses, lines, and rectangles), there are various ways to specify the position:

- A number without units is interpreted as that number of user units in the current coordinate system.

- Lengths *with* units are scaled according to the viewBox or transformations in effect. CSS px units are always interchangeable with SVG user units.

- Percentages are relative to the width or height specified in the viewBox of the nearest <svg> or <symbol> element (or the actual width and height, if no viewBox was given).

On a <text> element, both x and y default to 0 if not specified.

The default y="0" value can position text out of sight, above the top edge of the SVG, if the default top-left origin is used.

Any text content within an SVG that *isn't* inside a `<text>` element will not be displayed. This is in contrast to HTML, where text is printed to the screen by default.

 This behavior difference can be used within inline SVG (in HTML pages) to print a warning to the page for users of older browsers that don't support SVG. Text inside the `<svg>` but not inside a `<text>` will only be visible on these out-of-date browsers.

For short text labels, the x and y attributes may be the only positioning information you need. These values create an anchor point for the text. The browser aligns the first letter at this point and then types out the rest in a single row. Each letter is positioned next to the previous one, according to the normal spacing rules for the font and styles used.

Depending on how you are controlling the position of your graphic, x and y may not even be required. Coordinate system transformations also affect the position (and direction and scale) of text. The transformations can be applied to a parent `<g>` (grouping) element, or to the `<text>` element itself, as follows:

```
<text transform="translate(10,64)">SVG Text</text>
```

The x and y attributes default to 0, but the (0,0) origin point of the coordinate system has now been shifted 10 units left and 64 units down. Because SVG user units are interchangeable with px units, and the original SVG was 80 units tall, and 80% of 80 is 64, this positions the text in the exact same place as Figure 2-1.

Of course, you can combine `transform` with x and y, too. Just as with other SVG shapes, the positioning attributes are calculated in the transformed coordinate system. So any of these snippets would also align the text in the same position:

```
<text x="10px" transform="translate(0,64)">SVG Text</text>
<text y="80%" transform="translate(10,0)">SVG Text</text>
<text x="50px" y="-20%"
      transform="translate(-40,80)">SVG Text</text>
```

The `transform` attribute used in SVG 1 and 1.1 only accepts user-unit values for translations, so it is not as flexible as x and y; we needed to convert the units and percentages to user unit measurements. In contrast, the extended CSS `transform` property introduced by the CSS Transforms Module accepts lengths or percentages, or even `calc()` functions combining the two, but it does *not* allow lengths or angles to be written as numbers without units.

For optimal browser support, the SVG 1.1 syntax is recommended; CSS transforms on SVG elements are not supported in Internet Explorer, although they are planned for Microsoft Edge. Inconsistencies in other browsers are still being ironed out. Under the new CSS Transforms specification, the SVG 1.1 syntax (without units) will continue to be supported when used as an attribute.

This side of SVG text—attributes that set x and y positions, and transformations—is very similar to SVG shapes. Other text options used for SVG text are very similar to CSS-formatted HTML content.

Big Words, Little Words

The text in Example 2-1 used the browser's default text styles. Nothing in the code specifies what font to use, how large, or in what colors. In effect, it just says "write this text here."

The default `font-family` is entirely up to the browser or user defaults; it is usually a fairly innocuous, common font, but will differ from one program to another. The default `font-size` should be `medium`; on most browsers, this is equivalent to 16px. Unfortunately, this cannot be relied upon for many uses of SVG on the Web.

In all WebKit and Blink browsers prior to mid-2015, if you do not set a font size, it will default to 1px high when the SVG is embedded as an image (`<img>` element or CSS background image) inside HTML.

There is another reason to always set a font size for text within an SVG image. The text is being drawn in a custom coordinate system and will scale with the image. The ratio of the font size to the image size is kept constant, but the actual final font size on screen can vary.

In contrast, with HTML, you should always use the default root font size provided by the browser for body text. Headings and fine print can be made proportionally larger or smaller rather than given explicit values. This allows your design to adapt to user's settings, to make it accessible to those who cannot read small text.

The size of text in SVG is controlled by the familiar CSS `font-size` property. However, given SVG's flexible coordinate systems, the results of setting `font-size` may not always be what you expect.

There are two ways to set the `font-size` property—and most other style properties—in SVG. You can either use CSS rules with the same syntax as for HTML, or you can define the `font-size` attribute. The attribute is known as a *presentation attribute* and it participates in the CSS cascade as a rule with zero specificity. Except that it's actually less than zero: it can be overridden by the zero-specificity wildcard (`*`) selector!

Values set as a presentation attribute still inherit as normal, and still replace values inherited from parent elements. So in Example 2-2, the em-based `width` and `height` attributes on the `<svg>` will be calculated relative to the style rule `font-size`, but the actual text will be drawn at the size specified in the presentation attribute on the `<text>` element. The net result is shown in Figure 2-2.

Example 2-2. Defining font-size with style rules and presentation attributes

```
<svg xmlns="http://www.w3.org/2000/svg"
     xml:lang="en"
     width="24em" height="4.8em" viewBox="0 0 400 80" >
    <title>Font-size and SVG Text</title>
    <style type="text/css">
        svg { font-size: 12pt; }
    </style>
    <rect width="100%" height="100%" fill="lightYellow" />
    <text x="10px" y="80%" font-size="64px">SVG Text</text>
</svg>
```

SVG Text

Figure 2-2. Larger text in an SVG with font-relative dimensions

There are a number of ways you can specify font-size within CSS, all of which can also be used in SVG:

- As an absolute keyword, such as small, medium, or x-large. Much like t-shirts, your mileage may vary as to the precise values of these: browsers are allowed to decide exactly what these words mean. They should be the same (relative to the absolute measurements) in SVG as HTML.

- As a relative keyword, larger or smaller. Again, the amount of change is browser-dependent.

- As an absolute length with units (e.g., pt, mm, in).

- As a length in font-relative units (e.g., em, ex).

- As a percentage.

Length units introduced by the Values and Units Module Level 3 (ch, rem, and viewport units vw, vh, vmin, and vmax) can be used for font-size in SVG in all browsers that support them in general. The relative keywords, percentages, and all font-relative units are relative to the *inherited* font size.

 If you use the rem (root-em) unit in SVG graphics that will be used in HTML as images, be sure to explicitly set font-size on the root <svg> element to avoid the bug with root font-size in WebKit and Blink browsers.

For the font-size presentation attribute *only*, you may specify the font-size as a length in user units (e.g., as a number without units). For setting font size in a CSS rule, this will fail because the syntax is not valid for non-SVG content.

In CSS rules *or* presentation attributes, you can always use px as a synonym for user units.

As with all other lengths in SVG, the font-size you specify will be scaled according to the current coordinate system. An in will always be 96px and therefore 96 user units. A pt ($^1/_{72}$ of an inch) will always be $1^1/_3$px, and therefore $1^1/_3$ user units. Nontheless, these may be quite different from the print typographer's pt (point) unit or inches on a ruler.

Although all modern web browsers treat px as an absolute measurement, consistent with CSS 2.1, other SVG tools may scale px to the screen resolution or apply their own default resolution. For example, Inkscape used 90px per inch for many years, while Adobe Illustrator used 72px per inch.

For consistent results, set font-size in px if your SVG uses a viewBox to create a scaled user coordinate system—or if the SVG is sized in px directly. If your SVG is sized in absolute units (e.g., in or cm) and does not have a viewBox, use absolute units for the font size (e.g., pt or mm).

The coordinate system for a child element may be different from the coordinate system used by the parent—because of transformations or a new viewBox scale—so the size of letters on the screen may change even if the official font-size does not. Example 2-3 demonstrates this by drawing 6pt text in various coordinate systems, as shown in Figure 2-3.

Example 2-3. Using font-size in HTML and SVG

```
<!DOCTYPE html>
<html lang="en">
<head>
    <meta charset="utf-8" />
    <title>font-size and SVG Coordinate Systems</title>
    <style>
        body {
```

This is 6pt HTML text. It is very tiny and difficult to read.

Figure 2-3. A web page in which the SVG inherits the HTML font-size, but scales it differently

```
        background-color: lightYellow;
        font: 6pt sans-serif;                   ❶
    }
    svg {
        display: block;
        border: solid royalBlue;
        background-color: lightCyan;
        margin: 2em auto;
        width: 95%;
        max-width: 90vh;
        height: auto;
        min-height: 10em;
        max-height: 90vh;                        ❷
    }
</style>
```

```
</head>
<body>
    <p>This is 6pt HTML text.
      It is very tiny and difficult to read.</p>
    <svg viewBox="0 0 100 100">                            ❸
        <text x="5" y="1em">This is 6pt SVG text.</text>
        <text transform="translate(10,90) rotate(-30) scale(2,3)"
              >This is also 6pt text.</text>                ❹
    </svg>
</body>
</html>
```

❶ The font style rule on the HTML <body> element is the only point in the document that the font size is set.

❷ The remaining style rules ensure that the inline <svg> scales nicely to fit within the browser window—even if the browser does not support automatically scaling the SVG height to match the width and viewBox aspect ratio.

❸ The viewBox creates a square aspect ratio with 100 units in both the horizontal and vertical directions. This defines the basic scale used for the first <text> element.

❹ The second <text> element has a transform attribute that positions the text, rotates it, and then applies a non-uniform scale.

The font size in Figure 2-3 is always 8 units high in the current SVG coordinate system ($8=6\times1^1/_3$). When the coordinate system is unevenly scaled, the letters are stretched to match.

Future Focus
Non-Scaling Text and Other Vector Effects

When working with maps, diagrams, and data visualizations, a frequent desire is to have text *move* with the scale of the graphic, but not actually get any larger or smaller.

Currently, there are a few workarounds you can use to achieve this effect:

- Use JavaScript to calculate and control the scale of shapes and/or text, usually including adjusting the scale when the browser window changes.

- Use nested coordinate systems: enclose the graphics you wish to scale within a `<symbol>` or nested `<svg>` that has a **viewBox** and so will scale to fit; do not use a **viewBox** on the main SVG that contains the text, and instead position the text using percentages.

- Use a **viewBox** to scale the entire graphic to fit the screen size, then use CSS media queries to shrink the "official" **font-size** at larger screen sizes, canceling out the scaling effect.

None of these are ideal. A JavaScript solution impacts performance, and can be a lot of custom code if your graphic isn't drawn using JavaScript originally. Nested coordinate systems and percentage positions limit the benefits of using a **viewBox** in the first place: the percentage values will have no aspect ratio control. Media queries are fairly easy to use in standalone SVG files, but get complicated with inline SVG because the queries are based on the document size, not the SVG size.

The abandoned SVG 1.2 draft specification introduced the concept of *vector effects*: complex graphical manipulation instructions, similar to filter effects but applied on the vector definitions instead of the rasterized pixels. One of the options would have supported non-scaling text. However, the vector effect proposal as a whole proved too complex and resource intensive for most implementations at the time.

The current proposal for SVG 2 is to offer a limited number of the most requested vector effects using a list of keywords passed to the **vector-effects** property:

non-scaling-size
: The scale of units for this shape or text would be reset, without affecting the position; in addition to its use on text, it would be ideal for small icons and symbols in charts and graphs

non-scaling-stroke
: The **stroke-width** on shapes would always be calculated relative to the screen; for maps, this means that the lines on a map would stay the same size as you zoom in or out

non-rotation
: Any rotation or skew of the axes is reset, again without affecting the position of the origin

`fixed-position`

> The position of this element stays the same within the window, regardless of any transformations applied to the SVG; ideal for legends and user interface controls

Many of the details of how these effects would be implemented have not been decided at the time of writing, although experimental implementations of some values (particularly **non-scaling-stroke**) are available in some browsers.

Styling Text

There are many more styling options for text beyond setting its size. The following CSS 2 properties can be used to style SVG text:

- `font-family`, `font-size`, `font-size-adjust`, `font-stretch`, `font-style`, `font-variant`, and `font-weight` for selecting and scaling the font data
- `text-decoration` for adding underlines, overlines, and strikethroughs
- `text-transform` for converting to uppercase, lowercase, or capitalized words
- `direction` and `unicode-bidi` to control multidirectional language
- `letter-spacing` and `word-spacing` to adjust text spacing

At the time of writing, Firefox does not support `letter-spacing` and `word-spacing` for SVG text.

The `font-size-adjust` property is currently *only* supported in Firefox among major web browsers.

All of the properties just listed can be specified using either presentation attributes or style rules. Newer CSS 3 properties (introduced after the SVG 1.1 standard) may affect SVG text, but are less likely to be supported as attributes.

SVG also introduced a number of advanced text layout properties, which have since been adopted into or adapted by CSS 3 modules; these include the following: alignment-baseline, baseline-shift, dominant-baseline, glyph-orientation-horizontal, glyph-orientation-vertical, kerning, and writing-mode. Most of these will be discussed in Chapters 7 and 8. As detailed in those chapters, these properties are not well implemented in browsers; some will be deprecated in favor of CSS 3 alternatives.

One standard CSS text styling property that does *not* affect SVG text is color. In CSS-styled HTML, color sets the color of the text letters. However, in SVG text, the color is controlled by the same fill property you use to set the color of SVG shapes.

 If this seems like an unnecessary complication, be assured that it is because you have much more flexible options for coloring SVG text, as we'll discuss in Chapter 3.

Combining multiple effects, you could replace the basic text example from Example 2-1 with the following element and presentation attributes:

```
<text x="10" y="80%"
      font-family="Verdana, Geneva, sans-serif"
      font-size="64px"
      font-weight="bold"
      text-decoration="underline"
      fill="darkBlue"
      >SVG Text</text>
```

Alternatively, you could use the original <text> element and add a <style> element with the following rules:

```
text {
    font-family: Verdana, Geneva, sans-serif;
    font-size: 64px;
    font-weight: bold;
    text-decoration: underline;
    fill: darkBlue;
}
```

For optimal support in SVG tools other than web browsers, specify the stylesheet language by including a `type="text/css"` attribute on the `<style>` element.

Either version, presentation attributes or style rules, would create the text in Figure 2-4.

SVG Text

Figure 2-4. Styled SVG text

When using CSS (but not presentation attributes), you can also use the `font` property as a shorthand to set size and family together, along with other common options such as italic or bold. The shorthand for the same styles would look as follows:

```
text {
    font: bold 64px Verdana, Geneva, sans-serif;
    text-decoration: underline;
    fill: darkBlue;
}
```

The optional bold/italic values are specified first; both revert to `normal` if left out. The font size and at least one font-family value are required, and must be specified in that order.

Chapter 10 will discuss fonts and the `font-family` property in more detail, including the generic family keywords (such as `sans-serif`), system fonts (such as Verdana and Geneva), and web fonts.

So far, the text in the SVG examples has not looked that much different from text in HTML. However, the SVG text is also an SVG graphic, and can have graphical effects applied to it, such as transformations, filters, masks, and clipping paths. For example, many of the figures in Chapter 1 used a filter to create a puffed-up three-dimensional effect.

Example 2-4 provides the code for that filter and uses the `filter` property to apply it to our basic text example. Figure 2-5 shows the effect in action.

Example 2-4. Applying graphical effects to SVG text

```
<svg xmlns="http://www.w3.org/2000/svg"
    xml:lang="en"
    width="4in" height="0.8in" viewBox="0 0 400 80" >
    <title>Filter Effects on SVG Text</title>
    <style type="text/css">
        text {
            font: bold 64px Verdana, Geneva, sans-serif;
            text-decoration: underline;
            fill: darkBlue;
            stroke: indigo;
            filter: url(#shine);                                    ❶
        }
    </style>
    <defs>
        <filter id="shine">
            <feGaussianBlur in="SourceGraphic" stdDeviation="2"
                            result="blur"/>                         ❷
            <feColorMatrix values="1.5  0   0   0.5 0
                                    0   1.5  0   0.5 0
                                    0    0  1.5 0.5 0
                                    0    0   0   1  -0.5" />         ❸
            <feOffset dx="-2.5" dy="-1.5" />                        ❹
            <feComponentTransfer result="highlight">
                <feFuncA type="linear" amplitude="2" />            ❺
            </feComponentTransfer>
            <feComposite in="blur" in2="highlight"
                        operator="arithmetic"
                        k1="0" k2="1" k3="1" k4="0" />
            <feComposite in2="SourceGraphic" operator="atop" />  ❻
        </filter>
    </defs>
    <rect width="100%" height="100%" fill="lightYellow" />
    <text x="10" y="80%">SVG Text</text>
</svg>
```

❶ The text styles, including `fill`, `stroke`, and `filter`, are applied using a CSS rule.

❷ The `<filter>` element describes the sequence of processing steps that will convert the basic vector shape or text into its final appearance. Each step is a filter effect (`fe`), starting with `feGaussianBlur` to create a blurred copy of the source graphic.

❸ An `feColorMatrix` modifies the image created by the previous step; the matrix values lighten all the colors but decrease the alpha channel so that partially transparent regions will disappear completely.

❹ An `feOffset` element shifts the lightened, blurred layer up and to the left.

❺ An `feComponentTransfer` element with `feFuncA` modifies the alpha channel again, doubling the opacity. This resets some of the changes made previously, so that some areas return to full opacity, but does not affect areas that had their alpha drop to zero. The result of this step is given the name `highlight` so that it can be referenced in the next step.

❻ The `feComposite` elements each take two input layers and combine them with the specified operator. First, the blurred and highlight layers are added together. Then the combined effect is layered over top the source graphic and clipped to only include the parts that overlap opaque areas of the original.

Figure 2-5. Filtered SVG text

The `<text>` element itself in Example 2-4 uses the exact same markup as in the basic code in Example 2-1; all the effects are applied using style properties. Importantly, the text remains accessible as machine-readable character data to search engines, screen readers, and your browser's own text search ("Find") or copy-and-paste functions.

Future Focus
Advanced Text Formatting Options

The CSS 3 Text Decoration Module introduces new options for styling text, which will likely eventually apply to SVG as well:

Text shadows

A text shadow draws a blurred and/or offset copy of the text, in a chosen color, behind the main text. The **text-shadow** property accepts a comma-separated list of text shadows to be layered behind the text.

Emphasis marks

In some languages, emphasis is indicated by adding dots or accent marks next to each letter (as opposed to a solid underline). The **text-emphasis-style** property would set the mark to be used, while the **text-emphasis-color** would set its color; a **text-emphasis** shorthand would set both. A **text-emphasis-position** option would control the position of the marks relative to the characters. Because the position usually applies to an entire document based on the language used, it is not reset by the shorthand that applies emphasis to a particular string of text.

Text decoration options

The **text-decoration** property defined in CSS 2 (and adopted by SVG 1 and 1.1) allowed you to add an underline, overline, or line-through the text. The line was always straight and solid, and it was always the same color as the rest of the text. In SVG, this means that it has the same **fill** and **stroke** properties.

The new module makes **text-decoration** a shorthand property. The original options (type of line) can be set specifically with the **text-decoration-line** property. The line's color is set with **text-decoration-color**, while the **text-decoration-style** property controls whether the line is solid, dotted, dashed, wavy, or double thickness. Except for **wavy**, these options are all the same as the equivalent options for CSS borders.

Because text color in SVG is controlled by two properties (**fill** and **stroke**), not one (**color**), **text-decoration-color** is problematic. The SVG 2 specifications therefore introduce **text-decoration-fill** and **text-decoration-stroke**. At this time, it is not expected to be possible to specify these values in the **text-decoration** shorthand.

In both the old and new versions of `text-decoration`, the value is *not* inherited. Instead, the line from the parent element passes *through* any child text spans. Even if the child spans have a different text color, the line's color does not change unless the child element sets its own text-decoration line.

At the time of writing, `text-shadow` is supported in all the latest browsers for HTML text, and in all except Internet Explorer for SVG; however, there are bugs and limitations in the other browsers, particularly if the text is transformed, stroked, or painted with a gradient or pattern. The `text-decoration-*` options are supported in Firefox and Blink for HTML, but only by Firefox in SVG —and even then, without support for changing the line color.

Labeling a Graphic

Because this is a book specifically about SVG text, most of the examples will only contain text, and not graphics. There are practical applications for text-only SVG, as we will see. Some graphical effects cannot be created with CSS-styled HTML text. In some cases, new CSS specifications have extended the effect to HTML, but browser support is much better with SVG, as with filtered text like that in Figure 2-5.

Nonetheless, the most common use of text in SVG is to annotate an SVG graphic with machine-readable, easily editable text. This section works through the process of adding text to an image. We'll start with the graphic from Figure 2-6, a minimalist drawing of a lily native to the Rocky Mountain regions of North America.

The complete code for the drawing is 150 lines when neatly formatted, so we're not going to print it out here. For the purpose of adding text to the graphic, the most important aspect of the SVG is the coordinate system it uses. The `viewBox` is "0 0 400 500", so the origin is top-left and the entire graphic is 400 units wide and 500 units tall. The base of the stem is positioned at (100,450).

We start by adding a title and subtitle to the image, aligned with the base of the drawing:

```
<text role="heading" aria-level="1"
      x="170" y="450">Wood Lily</text>
```

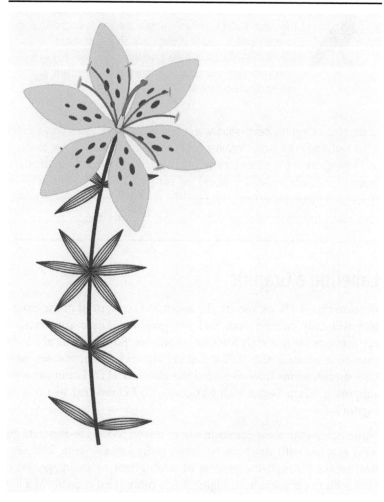

Figure 2-6. Drawing of a Western Wood Lily

```
<text xml:lang="la" role="heading" aria-level="2"
      x="190" y="480">Lilium montanum</text>
```

The text is then styled by a series of CSS rules:

```
text {
    font-family: Georgia, serif;
    font-size: 24px;
}
[role="heading"] {
    fill: darkSlateGray;
}
```

Wood Lily
Lilium montanum

Figure 2-7. Titled drawing of a Western Wood Lily

```
[role="heading"][aria-level="1"] {
    font-size: 48px;
}
:lang(la){
    font-style: italic;
}
```

The drawing with styled titles is shown in Figure 2-7.

The heading text is selected using an attribute selector, based on the value of the role attribute. The top-level and secondary headings are distinguished by the aria-level attribute. Although you could have used classes to apply the styles, the ARIA attribute adds meaning for accessible technologies that interpret your SVG content, such as screen readers.

Unlike HTML, SVG does not have any *semantic* (meaningful) elements that define the purpose of different text sections. There is no <h1> or <figcaption> that could convey the purpose of the text or give it a hierarchy. The role and aria-level attributes provide this structure.

The Accessible Rich Internet Applications (ARIA) attributes were developed by the W3C's Web Accessibility Initiative (WAI) to make it easier for accessible technologies to navigate multipart web pages and interact with JavaScript-controlled websites. SVG 2 explicitly adopts them for use in SVG, but most web browsers already support them.

Unfortunately, there are only a limited number of WAI-ARIA roles available to describe basic text features, such as paragraphs and emphasized words, that were already well defined in HTML. More nuanced roles may be available in future versions of ARIA.

Similarly, a semantic selector is used to apply the italic font style to the botanical name. The markup uses the xml:lang="la" attribute to identify the text as Latin, in contrast to the main language of the document, which is set to English using an xml:lang="en" attribute on the root <svg> element. The :lang(la) CSS pseudoclass selector then applies the style rules. Unlike an attribute selector, the :lang() selector not only applies to the element that has the language defined on it, but also to any child elements that inherit that language setting. Plus, it avoids the hassle of dealing with XML namespaces in CSS!

Text in an SVG need not be limited to a simple title. In data visualizations and diagrams, you may need multiple labels integrated carefully with the graphical content. Figure 2-8 shows one possible set of labels for the lily drawing, outlining the parts of the plant and flower structure. The labels have been made interactive, so the user can

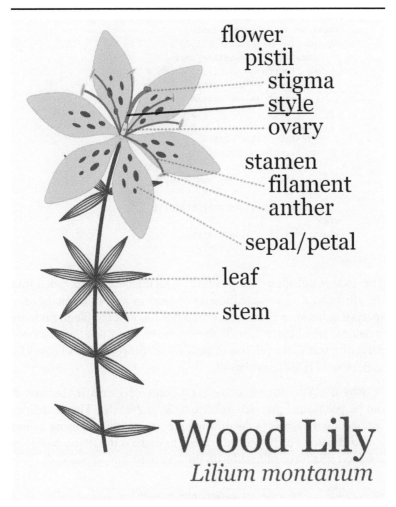

flower
pistil
stigma
style
ovary

stamen
filament
anther

sepal/petal

leaf

stem

Wood Lily
Lilium montanum

Figure 2-8. Labeled drawing of a Western Wood Lily, showing interactive highlighting of the word "style"

hover/focus each one and the label and connector line will both be highlighted.

The labels are structured using indentation to represent the structure of the parts being described. One way to represent this layout in SVG markup would be to re-create the nesting structure with group (<g>) elements and transformations:

```
<g class="labels" transform="translate(225,0)">
    <text y="1em">flower</text>
    <g transform="translate(25,0)">
        <text y="2em">pistil</text>
        <g transform="translate(25,0)">
            <text y="3em">stigma</text>
            <text y="4em">style</text>
            <text y="5em">ovary</text>
        </g>
        <text y="6.5em">stamen</text>
        <g transform="translate(25,0)">
            <text y="7.5em">filament</text>
            <text y="8.5em">anther</text>
        </g>
        <text y="10em">sepal/petal</text>
    </g>
    <text y="11.5em">leaf</text>
    <text y="13em">stem</text>
</g>
```

The code is not ideal. The position of each label is hard coded into the attribute; if you wanted to add or remove a label, or change the spacing in between them, you would need to edit the file in multiple locations. In Chapter 4, we'll show how you can position multiple parts of a text block relative to each other; however, it will never be as flexible as HTML text layout.

So why use SVG for structured text content? Primarily because it can be positioned precisely relative to SVG *graphics*. The guidelines connecting the labels to the drawing are also positioned using *x*- and *y*- coordinates. For the entire graphic to make sense, these positions need to remain coordinated with the text positions, at any scale.

In order to use em units to position the ends of the lines, the <line> elements must have the same font-size property as the <text> elements. The easiest way to do this is to set the font size on the parent <svg>.

A number of additional features are then integrated in the code to improve the accessibility of the text:

- Each text label is given an id value, so that it can be referenced in the aria-labelledby attribute of the corresponding graphic object.

- The text elements and groups have been given `role` attributes of `list` and `list-item` so that the nested structure is clearly communicated to screen readers; this requires extra `<g>` elements to combine the text label and its nested list in a single `list-item` element.

- The nested lists also have `aria-labelledby` attributes linking back to their headings, so they are clearly identified if the user jumps between content.

- In most browsers, the list items are made keyboard accessible by adding `focusable="true"` and `tabindex="0"` attributes using a script.

Example 2-5 provides the complete code for the text and guidelines.

Example 2-5. Positioning structured, interactive labels on a diagram

```
<svg xmlns="http://www.w3.org/2000/svg"
    xmlns:xlink="http://www.w3.org/1999/xlink"
    width="400" height="500" viewBox="0 0 400 500"
    xml:lang="en" aria-labelledby="title">
  <title>Wood Lily</title>
  <style type="text/css">
    /* Styles for main graphic omitted */
    svg {
        font-size: 24px;
    }
    text {
        font-family: Georgia, serif;
        fill: #123;
    }
    [role="heading"] {
        fill: darkSlateGray;
    }
    [role="heading"][aria-level="1"] {
        font-size: 48px;
    }
    :lang(la){
        font-style: italic;
    }
    line {
        stroke: #123;
        stroke-width: 2px;
        stroke-linecap: round;
        stroke-opacity: 0.3;
        stroke-dasharray: 1 3;
        transition: stroke-opacity 0.5s 0.1s,
                    stroke-dasharray 0.1s;
```

```
        }
        text:hover + line, text:focus + line {
            stroke-opacity: 0.8;
            stroke-dasharray: 7 0;
            transition: stroke-opacity 0.5s,
                        stroke-dasharray 0.4s 0.2s;
        }
        :focus {
            outline: none;
        }
        .labels text:hover,
        text:focus,
        g:focus > text:first-of-type {
            text-decoration: underline;
        }
    </style>
    <!-- Main graphics markup omitted -->
    <g id="title">
        <text role="heading" aria-level="1"
            x="170" y="450">Wood Lily</text>
        <text xml:lang="la" role="heading" aria-level="2"
            x="190" y="480">Lilium montanum</text>
    </g>
    <g class="labels" transform="translate(225,0)" role="list"
       aria-label="parts of the plant">
        <g role="listitem">
            <text id="flower" y="1em">flower</text>
            <g transform="translate(25,0)"
               role="list" aria-labelledby="flower">
                <g role="listitem">
                    <text id="pistil" y="2em">pistil</text>
                    <g transform="translate(25,0)"
                       role="list" aria-labelledby="pistil">
                        <text id="stigma" y="3em"
                              role="listitem">stigma</text>
                        <line x1="-5" y1="2.75em" x2="-130" y2="75"/>
                        <text id="style" y="4em"
                              role="listitem">style</text>
                        <line x1="-5" y1="3.75em" x2="-150" y2="100"/>
                        <text id="ovary" y="5em"
                              role="listitem">ovary</text>
                        <line x1="-5" y1="4.75em" x2="-155" y2="115"/>
                    </g>
                </g>
                <g role="listitem">
                    <text id="stamen-label" y="6.5em">stamen</text>
                    <g transform="translate(25,0)"
                       role="list" aria-labelledby="stamen">
                        <text id="filament" y="7.5em"
                              role="listitem">filament</text>
                        <line x1="-5" y1="7.25em" x2="-120" y2="145"/>
```

```
                        <text id="anther" y="8.5em"
                              role="listitem">anther</text>
                        <line x1="-5" y1="8.25em" x2="-112" y2="161"/>
                    </g>
                </g>
                <text id="sepal" y="10em"
                      role="listitem">sepal/petal</text>
                <line x1="-5" y1="9.75em" x2="-115" y2="175"/>
            </g>
        </g>
        <text id="leaf" y="11.5em" role="listitem">leaf</text>
        <line x1="-5" y1="11.25em" x2="-110" y2="270"/>
        <text id="stem" y="13em" role="listitem">stem</text>
        <line x1="-5" y1="12.75em" x2="-135" y2="305"/>
    </g>
    <script><![CDATA[
(function(){
    var items = document.querySelectorAll("[role='listitem']");
    for (var i=0, n=items.length; i<n; i++) {
        items[i].setAttribute("tabindex", 0);
        items[i].setAttribute("focusable", true);
    }
})();
]]></script>
</svg>
```

The `focusable` attribute, introduced in SVG Tiny 1.2, is only supported in Internet Explorer. The `tabindex` attribute, adopted for SVG 2 from HTML, is currently only supported for SVG in Blink/WebKit browsers.

To ensure broader keyboard accessibility in SVG, you could wrap each <text> element in an <a> link; these are keyboard focusable in most browsers by default.

CSS pseudoclass selectors trigger the changes in styles when text are moused-over or focused; CSS transitions animate the effect in browsers that support them for SVG content (i.e., except in IE). However, these interactive features will only apply if the SVG file is viewed directly or if it is embedded in a web page using an <object> element. If the SVG is embedded as an image, it will not receive any user events (also, the script will not execute). Alternatively, the SVG code could be copied into an HTML file directly as inline markup.

Future Focus
Automatically Positioned Connectors

The markup used to carefully position the labels and connecting lines in Example 2-5 is unfortunately repetitive and interdependent. Although the embased vertical positions make the layout flexible to changes in font size, other layout changes would require multiple coordinated edits. For example, because the `<line>` elements are nested inside the transformed groups, the horizontal positions of the other end point are dependent on the amount of indentation applied in each `transform` attribute.

A proposed extension to SVG would allow connecting lines to be specified by the *objects* they are attached to rather than by specific coordinates. Possible connection points could be assigned to each object (graphic or text) in their own coordinate system, and the connector would link the two regardless of how the objects are rearranged.

The SVG Connectors specification is not part of the core SVG 2 update, and the syntax and specific features have not been finalized at the time of writing.

CHAPTER 3

Colorful Language

The shape and size of SVG letters may be controlled by the standard CSS font selection properties, but the final appearance is uniquely SVG. As far as painting the text, letters are just another vector shape in SVG, defined by the Bézier curves within the vector font files. Results may be strange if you use a bitmap font, but those are few and far between on modern computers.

Like all SVG shapes, the paint of text is affected by two properties: fill for the interior, and stroke for the outline.

Fill and Stroke

The normal shape of a letter in an OpenType-compatible vector font is created by filling in the outlines from the font file. Therefore, for "normal" looking text in SVG, you set the fill property to a solid color. For more adventurous text, you can use gradient or patterned fills, or no fill at all, just a stroked outline.

Each glyph is painted individually, in logical reading order. If the text has a thick stroke, the overlap of each letter on previous ones may be visible. For cursive scripts, strokes are often unattractive because they highlight the edges of each glyph, counteracting the impression of a continuous stroke from one letter to the next.

As with every other shape in SVG, the default appearance for text is solid black fill and no stroke.

Both fill and stroke have the same allowed values:

- The keyword none
- A color value, using any CSS color format supported by the software—keywords, hex colors like #080844 or #fab, or functions like rgb(20, 100, 128) or hsla(0,80%,75%,0.7)
- A url() reference to the id of an SVG *paint server* (gradient or pattern element).

You can include a fallback color in addition to a paint server reference. It will be used if there is an error generating the gradient or pattern.

The SVG specifications also allow you to define colors based on the International Color Commission's ICC color profiles. For example, you could use Pantone named colors. These are mostly of use in print graphics, and are not supported in web browsers.

SVG's painting options can be used to dress up text within an HTML document. A short heading or title on a web page can be replaced by an inline SVG that draws the text. Example 3-1 uses this approach to create headings with the most basic of SVG-only effects: outlined letters. The final web page is displayed in Figure 3-1.

Example 3-1. Using SVG text to add graphical effects to HTML headings

```
<!DOCTYPE html>
<html>
<head>
    <meta charset="utf-8" />
    <title>SVG Text Headings</title>
    <style>
        body {
            background-color: #DEF;
            font-family: serif;
```

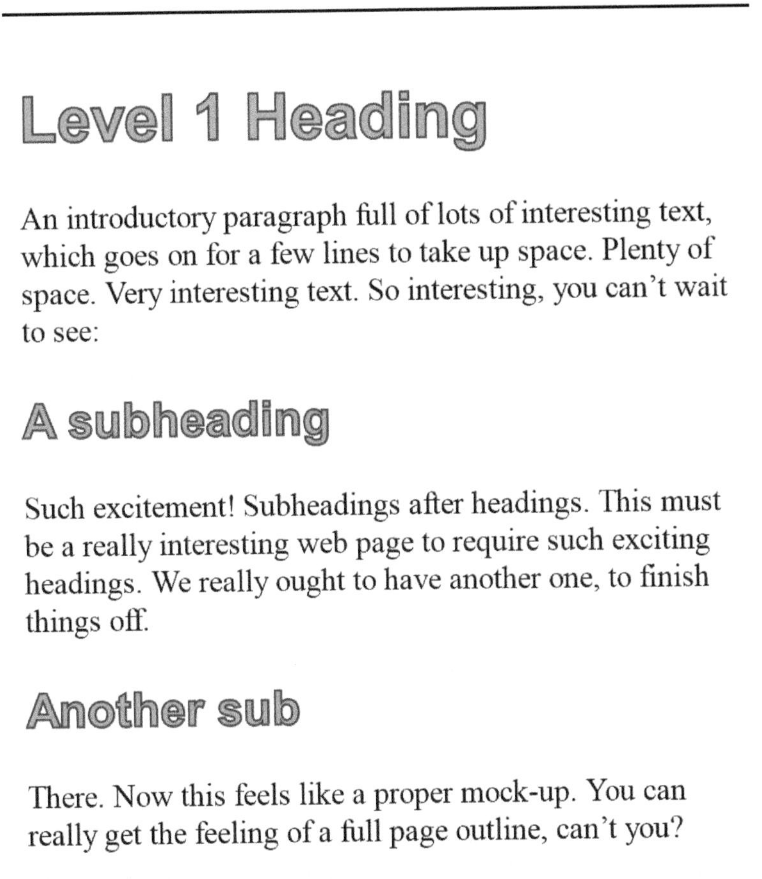

Level 1 Heading

An introductory paragraph full of lots of interesting text, which goes on for a few lines to take up space. Plenty of space. Very interesting text. So interesting, you can't wait to see:

A subheading

Such excitement! Subheadings after headings. This must be a really interesting web page to require such exciting headings. We really ought to have another one, to finish things off.

Another sub

There. Now this feels like a proper mock-up. You can really get the feeling of a full page outline, can't you?

Figure 3-1. A web page with SVG text headings

```
}
h1 svg, h2 svg {
    width: 80%;
    height: 1em;                      ❶
    display: inline-block;
    vertical-align: baseline;         ❷
    overflow: visible;
    padding-bottom: 0.4em;
    margin-bottom: -0.4em;            ❸
}
h1, h2 {
    font-family: sans-serif;
    stroke: darkRed;                  ❹
}
h1 {
```

```
        fill: coral;
    }
    h2 {
        fill: lightCoral;
    }
    </style>
</head>
<body>
    <h1><svg role="presentation">                    ❺
        <text y="1em">Level 1 Heading</text>      ❻
    </svg></h1>
    <p>An introductory paragraph full of lots of interesting text,
    which goes on for a few lines to take up space.  Plenty of
    space.  Very interesting text.  So interesting, you can't wait
    to see:
    </p>
    <h2><svg role="presentation">
        <text y="1em">A subheading</text></svg></h2>
    <p>Such excitement!  Subheadings after headings.  This must be
    a really interesting web page to require such exciting headings.
    We really ought to have another one, to finish things off.
    </p>
    <h2><svg role="presentation">
        <text y="1em">Another sub</text></svg></h2>
    <p>There.  Now this feels like a proper mock-up.  You can really
    get the feeling of a full page outline, can't you?
    </p>
</body>
</html>
```

❶ The <svg> elements within each heading are set to take up the
   full available width and one line of text's height (1em). Exactly
   how high that is will depend on the inherited font-size values.
   In this case, those will be the browser default font sizes for <h1>
   and <h2>.

❷ The SVG will create an inline block that sits on the normal text
   baseline for the heading text. The text will then be adjusted to
   sit along the bottom of the SVG.

❸ Because this means that the descenders of letters will extend
   outside the <svg>, it has overflow set to visible. Because Web-
   Kit and older Blink browsers won't draw inline SVG content
   outside of the padding region, some extra padding is added and
   then canceled out with a negative margin.

❹ The styles for the headings are set directly on the <h1> and <h2> elements; they will inherit into the SVG.

❺ The markup for the headings is very simple: the heading text is inside a <text> element, inside an <svg>, within the HTML heading markup. The ARIA presentation role tells assistive technologies to ignore the SVG markup, because it is only there for stylistic effect. The text content of the SVG will still be recognized, with its role defined by the HTML heading elements.

❻ One positioning attribute is required: the y value that shifts the text from sitting on the top edge of the SVG to sitting on the bottom edge.

One important limitation of using SVG for HTML headings is that the layout will not automatically adjust for narrow screens. HTML text in a CSS block element would wrap to a new line if it reaches the edge of the content area. SVG text, in contrast, will keep typing in a straight line off the edge of the screen.

As we'll see in future chapters, multiline SVG text is possible, but browsers do not yet support automatically wrapping text. Even if they did, that would not automatically cause the parent <svg> element to expand to make room.

Future Focus
Outlined Text Outside of SVG

The ability to create outlined letters, similar to SVG stroked text, has been considered repeatedly in CSS. Early drafts of the CSS 2 specification included a text-outline property, along with text-shadow, which would have allowed solid or blurred outlines. Both were dropped because of implementation problems. Shadows have been readopted in CSS 3, but outlines—after a brief resurgence—have been dropped again.

WebKit-based browsers (including Blink browsers) support the non-standard -webkit-text-stroke property. It is closer to SVG stroking than the text-outline proposal, in that it does not support blurred outlines, and the strokes are centered over the edges of the letters, not on the outside.

Given the widespread support for **text-shadow** in modern browsers, many web designers have taken to faking an outline by layering together lightly blurred text-shadows, offset in many different directions. The inefficiency of using four or eight text shadows to mimic one text outline has so far not convinced browser makers to adopt the previous proposal.

It is quite possible that, instead of creating a separate property, CSS will choose to expand **text-shadow**. The similar **box-shadow** property allows you to make the shadow larger than the box. If the same "spread" parameter was supported for text shadows, it would have the same effect as the original **text-outline** proposal.

Because the text content of the inline SVGs is contained *inside* the HTML heading markup, there is no need for extra ARIA attributes to explain how the SVG text formatting relates to the document outline. In fact, in a browser that does not support inline SVG, the SVG elements would be ignored and the text would be treated as normal HTML heading text.

However, those HTML headings would not be colored, because the color was set using the SVG-specific properties `fill` and `stroke`. If you wanted the heading text to show up in red or orange on Internet Explorer 8, you would need to also set the `color` property.

Manually coordinating two different properties like this leaves room for error. If you want to match a color in the SVG with the color of the HTML text that it is embedded in, you can instead use the `currentColor` keyword.

Coordinating Colors

The `currentColor` keyword always evaluates to the value of the `color` property in effect for the element. It was originally introduced in CSS to represent the default behavior of borders, which match text color if not otherwise set.

For SVG, the most important use of `currentColor` is to coordinate inline icons with surrounding text. Example 3-2 uses `currentColor` to create icons that provide extra information about the destination of a hyperlink. The icons change color with the rest of the hyperlink.

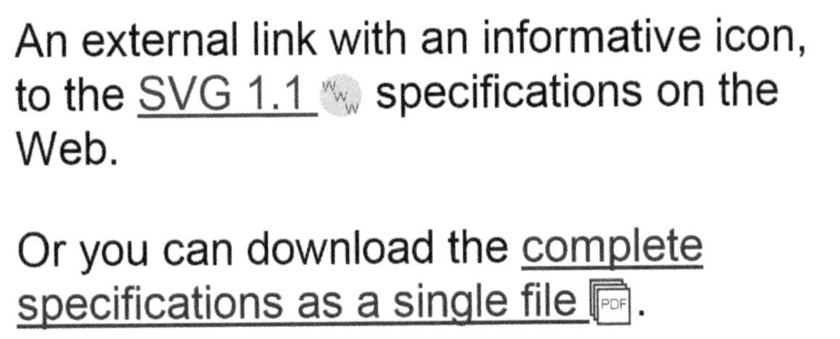

An external link with an informative icon, to the <u>SVG 1.1</u> <span title="icon">ⓦ</span> specifications on the Web.

Or you can download the <u>complete specifications as a single file</u> 🄿🄳🄵.

Figure 3-2. SVG icons that match the color of the surrounding HTML text

Figure 3-2 shows the resulting HTML content as it appears with default browser link colors in Firefox.

Example 3-2. Using currentColor to create SVG content that matches HTML

```html
<!DOCTYPE html>
<html lang="en">
<head>
    <meta charset="utf-8" />
    <title>Color-Matching Icons</title>
    <style>
        body {
            background-color: #DEF;
            font-family: sans-serif;
            font-size: x-large;
        }
        svg.icon {
            display: inline-block;
            height: 1em;
            width: 1em;
            vertical-align: text-bottom;          ❶
        }
        svg.defs {
            display: block;
            position: absolute;
            left: -10;
            height: 0; width: 0;                  ❷
        }
    </style>
</head>
```

```
<body>
    <svg class="defs" aria-hidden="true"
        focusable="false" width="0" height="0">
        <symbol id="external-link" viewBox="-10 -10 20 20">          ❸
            <circle r="9.5"
                    fill="currentColor" fill-opacity="0.3" />
            <g fill="currentColor" font-size="6">
                <text x="-8" y="-2" >W</text>
                <text x="-3" y="3" >W</text>
                <text x="2" y="8" >W</text>
            </g>
        </symbol>
        <symbol id="pdf" viewBox="0 0 20 20">                         ❹
            <rect id="r" x="0.5" y="0.5" width="14" height="15"
                    fill="white" stroke="currentColor" />
            <use xlink:href="#r" x="1.5" y="2" />
            <use xlink:href="#r" x="3" y="4" />
            <text x="5" y="13" fill="currentColor"
                    font-size="6">PDF</text>
        </symbol>
    </svg>
    <p>An external link with an informative icon, to the
    <a href="http://www.w3.org/TR/SVG11/Overview.html">SVG 1.1
        <svg class="icon">                                           ❺
            <use xlink:href="#external-link">
                <title>External link</title>
            </use>
        </svg></a>
        specifications on the Web.</p>
    <p>Or you can download the
        <a href="http://www.w3.org/TR/SVG11/REC-SVG11-20110816.pdf"
            >complete specifications as a single file
        <svg class="icon">
            <use xlink:href="#pdf">
                <title>PDF file</title>
            </use>
        </svg></a>.</p>
</body>
</html>
```

❶ The icon class will be applied to individual inline <svg> elements, and ensures they will be 1em-square elements that align nicely with the surrounding text.

❷ The defs class applies to a single inline SVG that holds all the definitions for the icon symbols. The CSS styles ensure that this element does not affect the web page layout or appearance.

❸ The first icon will be used to mark links to external websites. It consists of the letters "WWW" overlaid on a semitransparent circle, both filled with the current text color.

❹ The second icon will be used to mark links to PDF files. It consists of the letters "PDF" written on a set of stacked rectangles to represent a multipage document. The letters are filled with the current text color; the pages are white but have a matching colored outline.

❺ The icons are used by inserting a small block of inline SVG code directly, contained within each `<a>` link in the HTML.

The `currentColor` keyword can be used anywhere in SVG that a color value is needed. In Example 3-2, it is used as both `fill` and `stroke` color within the icon symbols. The symbols inherit styles— including the `color` setting—from the `<use>` elements, which inherit them from the links. Links are by default colored in web browsers, with different colors depending on whether that link has previously been visited or is actively being selected.

Because the visited status of a link can reveal personal information about a user, browsers may hide the information about a link color from any place it could be accessed by web page scripts.

In Blink browsers, this is implemented in a way that prevents the `:visited` link color from being inherited using the `currentColor` keyword: the icon is always blue, not purple. Other color changes (such as the red `:active` link state when the link is clicked) *are* propagated to the icon.

Because the icons express additional information, that information is also made available as accessible text. The `<title>` element is used so that the accessible text is also available to other uses as a tooltip— in case the meaning of our super-simple icons is unclear!

The `<title>` element is a child of the `<use>` element, not of the `<svg>`. Many browsers do not create tooltips for a `<title>` that is the direct child of an `<svg>`, even when that SVG is inline in HTML.

When an SVG is viewed as its own file, its title appears in the browser's tab or title bar, so a tooltip is not required.

By grouping symbol definitions in a single <svg>, they can be reused as often as necessary, without cluttering the main document markup with SVG tags. The nested <svg>, <use>, and <title> elements are only slightly more complicated than an <img> element—but the end result is considerably more flexible, a stylable graphic that is part of the main document.

Avoid using display: none to hide the definitions <svg>. Although this *should* work according to the specifications, in practice, browsers will not properly render reused content that has a parent with display: none. In particular, gradients and patterns will not work in any current browser, and some browsers may not draw reused graphics, particularly if those graphics are not part of a <symbol>.

The workaround is to use CSS absolute positioning properties to visually hide the content while still having it set to be "displayed." An aria-hidden="true" attribute ensures that it is also hidden from screen readers. A focusable="false" attribute ensures that it does not recieve keyboard focus in Internet Explorer, which implemented the SVG 1.2 focusable attribute and sets all <svg> elements to receive keyboard focus by default. (In other browsers and SVG 2, the tabindex attribute identifies focusable elements, and <svg> is *not* focusable by default.)

Some other things to note about the code in Example 3-2:

- The SVG icons are sized using em units, so that they scale to match the text in size as well as color. Because 1em is the height from the very top to the very bottom of letters, the vertical-alignment setting ensures that the bottom of the icon lines up with the bottom of the text (the lowest descending letters), rather than sitting on the text baseline.

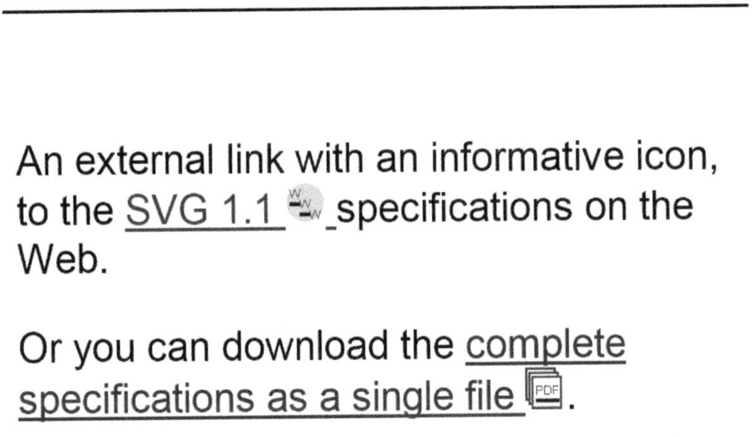

An external link with an informative icon, to the SVG 1.1 ⅏ specifications on the Web.

Or you can download the complete specifications as a single file 🗎.

Figure 3-3. SVG icons in a web page with careless CSS

- The SVG icons are set to `inline-block` mode instead of the default `inline`. Although this doesn't usually make a difference (an SVG is always a block), it ensures that the underline on the `<a>` elements isn't continued through the text within the icon. Whether this should ever happen is debatable; Internet Explorer never propagates an HTML underline through the SVG text, but Firefox and Blink/WebKit browsers do.

To demonstrate the importance of those points, Figure 3-3 shows the same page (in Firefox) if the definition SVG is set to zero height and width but not absolutely positioned—resulting in a blank line at the top of the page—and the icons are left with the default `inline` display mode and `baseline` vertical alignment.

Coordinating with HTML color is not the only benefit of `currentColor`. The keyword also offers flexibility when customizing the styles on content reused with the `<use>` element. Your reused content can inherit a `fill` value, a `stroke` value, and a `color` value, which can be used to set fill and/or stroke of particular parts of the icon. In the future, inheritable CSS variables will add even more flexibility, but for now, `color` and `currentColor` act as an extra variable for SVG styling.

However, one limitation of currentColor is that it will always be just that: a color. In contrast, SVG fill and stroke can use paint servers as well.

Painted Effects

SVG paint servers are separate elements (<linearGradient>, <radialGradient>, or <pattern>) that define a rectangle of graphic content. That content is then used to determine the color values for each point within the fill or outline of another shape—or text—that references the paint server in the fill or stroke property.

Paint servers can create many different graphical effects. A full discussion is outside the scope of this book,[1] but the possibilities are worth mentioning simply because they are one of the key benefits of using SVG text.

Example 3-3 showcases a simple effect: a gradient that fades to transparent across the width of the text. Figure 3-4 shows the result. Although you can't see the last (essentially transparent) letter, it is still there and can be selected if you copy and paste the text, or search for the words.

Example 3-3. Filling SVG text with paint server content

```
<svg xmlns="http://www.w3.org/2000/svg"
     xmlns:xlink="http://www.w3.org/1999/xlink"
     xml:lang="en"
     height="50px" width="410px">
    <title>Gradient-Filled Text</title>
    <defs>
        <linearGradient id="fade">
            <stop stop-color="black" stop-opacity="1" offset="0"/>
            <stop stop-color="black" stop-opacity="0" offset="1"/>
        </linearGradient>
    </defs>
    <g transform="translate(10,40)"
       style="font-family: Arial;
              font-weight: bold;
              font-size: 24pt;
              fill: url('#fade');">
        <text>A Whiter Shade of Pale</text>
```

---

1 A full discussion of paint servers is actually a book in itself: *SVG Colors, Patterns & Gradients* (O'Reilly), by the same authors as this book.

```
    </g>
</svg>
```

A Whiter Shade of

Figure 3-4. Black-to-transparent gradient as text fill

Gradient-filled text is another reason you might want to use SVG text to replace HTML headings. There are no cross-browser standard methods to fill HTML text with a gradient or image, although there are various workarounds available, using the non-standard `-webkit-background-clip: text` option (only available in WebKit/Blink browsers) or the (relatively new) CSS blending modes.

Example 3-4 adapts Example 3-1 to use gradient effects on the SVG heading text, for both fill and stroke; unchanged code is omitted to save space. The gradients used are more subtle than the fade-to-transparent effect; we are, after all, trying to keep the text legible. Figure 3-5 shows the end result.

Example 3-4. Using SVG gradients within HTML headings

```
<!DOCTYPE html>
<html lang="en">
<head>
    <meta charset="utf-8" />
    <title>SVG Gradient Text Headings</title>
    <style>
        /* basic layout styles unchanged */

        h1, h2 {
            font-family: sans-serif;
            color: coral;
            fill: url(#coral-gradient) currentColor;      ❶
        }
        h1 {
            stroke: url(#red-gradient) darkRed;           ❷
        }
        svg.defs {
          " display: block;
            position: absolute;
            left: -10;
            height: 0; width: 0;                          ❸
        }
```

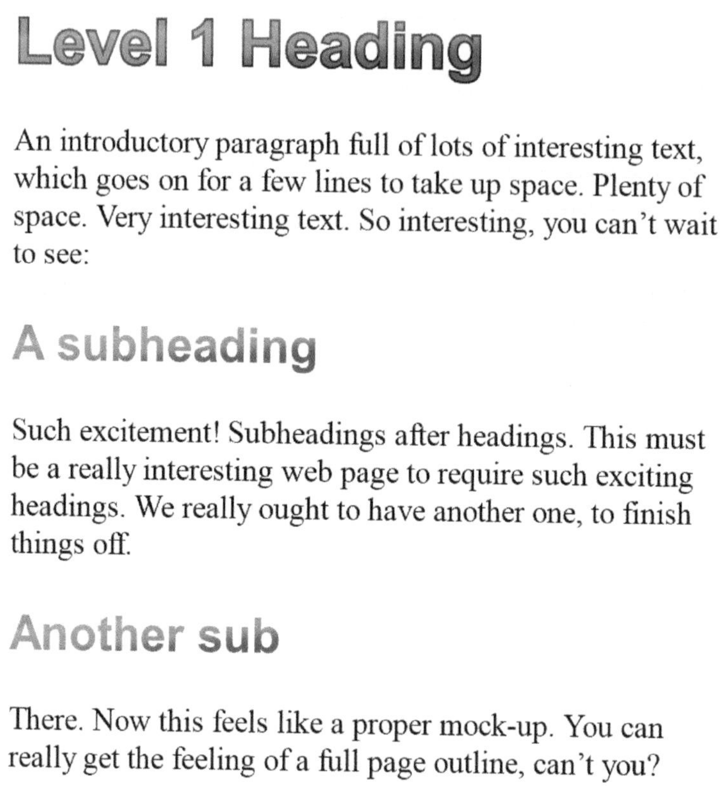

Level 1 Heading

An introductory paragraph full of lots of interesting text, which goes on for a few lines to take up space. Plenty of space. Very interesting text. So interesting, you can't wait to see:

A subheading

Such excitement! Subheadings after headings. This must be a really interesting web page to require such exciting headings. We really ought to have another one, to finish things off.

Another sub

There. Now this feels like a proper mock-up. You can really get the feeling of a full page outline, can't you?

Figure 3-5. HTML page with gradient-filled SVG text headings

```
      </style>
  </head>
  <body>
      <svg class="defs" aria-hidden="true"
          focusable="false" width="0" height="0">
          <linearGradient id="coral-gradient"
                      y2="100%" x2="50%" >             ❹
              <stop offset="0.3" stop-color="tomato" />
              <stop offset="0.4" stop-color="lightCoral" />
              <stop offset="0.7" stop-color="tomato" />
              <stop offset="0.9" stop-color="crimson" />
          </linearGradient>
          <linearGradient id="red-gradient"
                      xlink:href="#coral-gradient"> ❺
              <stop offset="0.3" stop-color="darkRed" />
```

```
        <stop offset="0.4" stop-color="red" />
        <stop offset="0.7" stop-color="darkRed" />
        <stop offset="0.9" stop-color="#400" />
    </linearGradient>
</svg>
<h1><svg role="presentation">
    <text y="1em">Level 1 Heading</text>
</svg></h1>
<!-- remaining markup is unchanged -->
</body>
</html>
```

❶ The headings will all have the same `fill` gradient. The `color` property and `currentColor` keyword are used to define a single fallback color for when SVG isn't supported or when there is a problem with the gradient.

❷ The top-level heading text will also have a gradient in the stroke, with a contrasting fallback color.

❸ All these gradients will be defined in their own `<svg>` definitions element, which is hidden using the same styles (and `aria-hidden` attribute) as Example 3-2.

❹ Attributes on the `<linearGradient>` element define the gradient position, from the default (0,0) position (top-left corner) to the midpoint of the bottom of the text area. The child `<stop>` elements define the color transition.

❺ The second gradient uses the `xlink:href` attribute to reference the first one; the first one is used as a template, and all of its attributes are copied over. This makes it easier to coordinate the two matching gradients, as the positioning attributes are only written once.

The bounding box used to size the gradient or pattern is based on the layout boxes (*em boxes*) for each character, including room on top for accents and below for descending letter. Many characters do not fill the entire em box. Some characters may even extend beyond it, particularly in decorative calligraphic fonts. The entire letter will still be filled, but the exact scale and position of the gradient or pattern may not be what you expect.

If the paint server uses userSpaceOnUse units, defining it in its own <svg> element, as in Example 3-4, will not work in many browsers. Firefox is the only browser (at the time of writing) that correctly applies the user space coordinate system from the filled or stroked content, instead of from the gradient's parent SVG.

As mentioned earlier in the chapter, using SVG to create decorative HTML headings should only be used if you know you will not need the text to wrap to a new line.

New Fill and Stroke Options

SVG 2 expands the options for **fill** and **stroke** to be more similar to CSS 3 backgrounds. You will be able to specify layers of multiple gradients or patterns. CSS gradient functions will be usable instead of references to SVG gradient elements, and separate image files will be usable as well. It should also be possible to control the size of each layer, again similar to CSS backgrounds.

CSS gradient functions and repeating image fills will replace many uses of SVG gradients and pattern. However, new SVG paint servers will add even more options. Mesh gradients will allow nearly infinite customization of smoth transitions of color. Hatches will make it much easier to create stripes, ripples, and cross-hatch patterns.

One SVG 2 feature already supported in some browsers is the ability to swap the order of fill and stroke. In SVG 1.1, strokes are always painted "on top" of the fill. For text, this means that thick strokes obscure the details of the letters. Swapping the order creates a neater outline effect, similar to a solid shadow or the text-outline that had been proposed for CSS.

The relevant property is called **paint-order**, and it takes an ordered list of the keywords **fill**, **stroke**, and **markers**. The order is translated into the painting order, from bottom to top, with any missing values filled in afterward in default order. In other words, **paint-order: stroke** is enough to ensure that strokes do not obscure the fill.

However, paint-order only controls the order of fill and stroke, per glyph. Each glyph is still painted individually, and strokes from one glyph may overlap the

---

previous one. A separate property may be adopted in the future to control this aspect of paint order.

Switching Styles

The examples so far have used a single set of styles for a complete <text> element. In order to apply different styles to *part* of the text, you can wrap the relevant characters in a <tspan> element. Like an HTML <span>, the <tspan> can be used to change color or font properties.

Example 3-5 uses styled <tspan> elements to change the colors and font of individual words within a <text> element, as displayed in Figure 3-6.

Example 3-5. Using tspan elements to change the formatting of SVG text

```
<svg xmlns="http://www.w3.org/2000/svg"
    xml:lang="en" width="10cm" height="2cm">
    <title>Formatting Text Spans</title>
    <style type="text/css">
        svg {
            font-family: serif;
            font-size: 12mm;
            fill: navy;
        }
    </style>
    <rect fill="#CEE" width="100%" height="100%" />
    <text x="5mm" y="1.5cm" >One,
        <tspan fill="royalBlue">Two,</tspan>
        <tspan font-style="italic" fill="royalBlue" stroke="navy"
            >Three!</tspan>
    </text>
</svg>
```

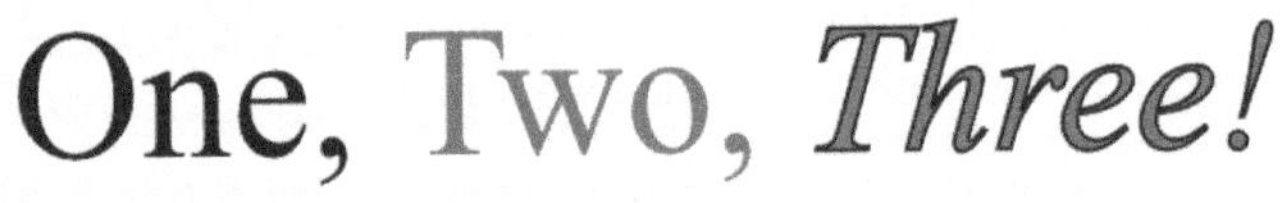

One, Two, *Three!*

Figure 3-6. SVG text with changing styles

As with the rest of SVG, styles on a `<tspan>` may be specified as presentation attributes or as CSS rules. Example 3-5 uses CSS rules to set default styles for the entire graphic, and then sets more specific values on the individual `<tspan>` elements with attributes—which always override inherited values, even when those values were originally set with CSS.

When restyling a `<tspan>` with paint server fill or stroke, the bounding box used to scale the paint server is based on the entire `<text>` element, not the individual `<tspan>`. For example, if we wanted to emphasize part of the gradient headings used in Example 3-4, we could add markup like the following:

```
<h1><svg role="presentation">
    <text y="1em">Level <tspan class="digit">1</tspan>
                Heading</text>
</svg></h1>
```

The class would be referenced in the following style rule to fill in the digit in the same dark red gradient used for the stroke:

```
h1 .digit {
    fill: url(#red-gradient) darkRed;
}
```

The result is shown in Figure 3-7. The angle and position of all three gradients—the fill on the main text, the fill on the `<tspan>`, and the stroke on both—align perfectly to create a continuous reflective effect.

Level 1 Heading

Figure 3-7. A different gradient fill within a single span of text

The continuous paint is one reason for using a `<tspan>` within a larger `<text>` element. However, even when using solid-colored fill, a `<tspan>` can make your work much smoother.

If you used three individual `<text>` elements to set the individual words in Example 3-5, you would then have to figure out the exact horizontal position for each word. Changing the presentation of text using `<tspan>`, in contrast, does not disrupt the continuous line of

text. Each character is still positioned based on the position of the previous character.

Nonetheless, in many cases you *do* want to disrupt or reset the position of characters within a line of text. A `<tspan>` can do that as well, as Chapter 4 will show.

Multiline SVG Text

A single SVG <text> element creates a single line of text. It does not—in SVG 1.1, anyway—have any way of wrapping text to a new line. For this reason, when text consists of more than independent short labels, individual <text> elements positioned at explicit points on the page are usually insufficient.

For longer text, you need to break the text into smaller chunks to position them separately. However, you often still want to coordinate the position of different words to reflect that they are part of a continuous whole. This is true not only for normal paragraph-like text wrapping, but also for an area in which SVG excels: complex text layouts used in posters, advertisements, and poetry.

Individual spans of SVG text can be shifted from their natural position, or repositioned completely. This chapter discusses the basic attributes to position spans of text, showing how you can move the virtual typewriter to a new point on the page. However, many style options affect the final position of the characters, and the following chapters will introduce these complexities.

Stepping Up

The <tspan> element can be used to identify segments of text for positioning as well as for styling. By default, each <tspan> is aligned next to the previous character in the text string, but attributes can reset or adjust that position.

Although a `<tspan>` element can be positioned independently, it cannot be used on its own: it must be inside a `<text>` element, which declares a block of SVG text.

There are four positioning attributes for SVG text: the x and y that we have already seen, and also dx and dy. While the first two declare absolute positions within the coordinate system, the latter two declare differences (or *deltas*) in position, which should be added to the position that otherwise would apply.

Any or all of these attributes can be applied to both `<text>` and `<tspan>` elements. Which to use depends on whether later parts of text should adjust if you change previous parts. If a `<tspan>` element has both x and y attributes, it is positioned independently of the previous content in the `<text>` element—and of the x and y attributes on the `<text>` itself.

Using a single `<text>` element provides a logical grouping—combining different pieces of text into a continuous whole—even if each `<tspan>` is positioned independently. This can affect copy-and-paste operations, screen readers, and search engine optimization.

Because x and y are independent attributes, you can control the position along one axis while letting the other axis be calculated automatically based on the text flow. The default x/y behavior for `<tspan>` is automatic positioning, in contrast to `<text>` elements, where these attributes default to 0.

Example 4-1 uses the y attribute to offset the vertical position of words within a text string. It uses the same text content and styles as Example 3-5. However, classes are used to set the styles so they don't distract from the geometric attributes in the markup. Figure 4-1 shows the result.

Example 4-1. Resetting the position of text using absolute attributes on tspan elements

```
<svg xmlns="http://www.w3.org/2000/svg"
     xml:lang="en" width="10cm" height="2.5cm">
```

```
<title>Positioning tspan</title>
<style type="text/css">
    svg {
        font-family: serif;
        font-size: 12mm;
        fill: navy;
    }
    .em {
        fill: royalBlue;
    }
    .strong {
        stroke: navy;
        font-style: italic;
    }
</style>
<rect fill="#CEE" width="100%" height="100%" />
<text x="5mm" y="2.1cm" >One,
    <tspan class="em" y="1.6cm">Two,</tspan>
    <tspan class="strong em" y="1.1cm">Three!</tspan>
</text>
</svg>
```

Figure 4-1. SVG text using automatic horizontal positions with absolute vertical positions

The exact same result can also be achieved using the *relative* positioning attributes, as follows:

```
<text x="5mm" y="2.1cm" >One,
    <tspan class="em" dy="-0.5cm">Two,</tspan>
    <tspan class="strong em" dy="-0.5cm">Three!</tspan>
</text>
```

The first dy shifts the current text position from 2.1cm to 1.6cm; the second span then starts from that position and the dy value shifts it up another half centimeter.

The <text> element as a whole is still positioned absolutely, but the <tspan> elements are positioned using dy to specify vertical offsets, instead of y to specify the final destination. The main benefit of using dy and dx is that you can move the entire element as a whole by changing the initial position value. All the pieces maintain their relative position.

Using dy and dx also allows you to specify the position of your text as a mix of length and percentage units. When an element (<text> or <tspan>) has both absolute and relative position attributes for a given direction (horizontal or vertical), the delta adjustments are applied *after* moving to the absolute position. You can therefore set the base position (x or y) using a percentage, then offset it by a fixed amount using dx or dy.

To ensure that the text from Example 4-1 always remains vertically centered within the SVG—even after changing the SVG height—you could position the original <text> element as an offset from 50%:

```
<text x="5mm" y="50%" dy="0.85cm">One,
    <tspan class="em" dy="-0.5cm">Two,</tspan>
    <tspan class="strong em" dy="-0.5cm">Three!</tspan>
</text>
```

In contrast, if you wanted the text to maintain its position relative to the *bottom* of the SVG (100% height), you would use the following:

```
<text x="5mm" y="100%" dy="-0.4cm">One,
    <tspan class="em" dy="-0.5cm">Two,</tspan>
    <tspan class="strong em" dy="-0.5cm">Three!</tspan>
</text>
```

Figure 4-2 shows the difference by embedding both versions of the SVG in an HTML page with <object> elements. Width and height set on the <object> with CSS are propagated to the SVG, overriding the dimensions set in the SVG file:

```
object {
    display: table-cell;
    width: 9.5cm;
    height: 2.5cm;
    margin: 0.25cm;
}
.stretch object {
    height: 7.5cm;
}
.squish object {
    height: 1.5cm;
}
```

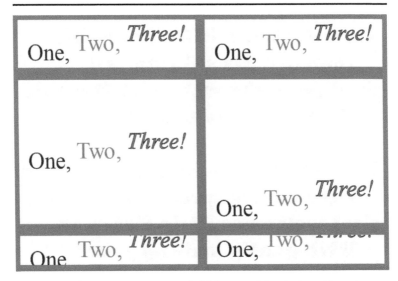

Figure 4-2. Percentage-positioned SVG text with relative offsets, in SVG objects of differing heights: positioned relative to 50% (left), positioned relative to 100% (right)

Because the SVG files (which are identical to Example 4-1 except for the text positioning attributes) do not have a `viewBox` attribute, the content does not scale. The percentages are calculated relative to the applied height and width.

In both cases, the adjustments on the `<tspan>` elements do not change. The effect of a `dy` attribute is always calculated from the final position of the previous text, regardless of whether that position was set with `y`, `dy`, or a combination of the two.

 SVG 2 is expected to adopt the CSS `calc()` function, which will make percentage-plus-offset adjustments possible within any length attribute.

The preceding examples have all used the natural flow of the text to control horizontal position. However, for many uses of SVG text, you'll need to reset the horizontal position with `x` and `dx` attributes. A `dx` value is also calculated from the final net position of previous text, including (for horizontal text) the offsets caused by the letters

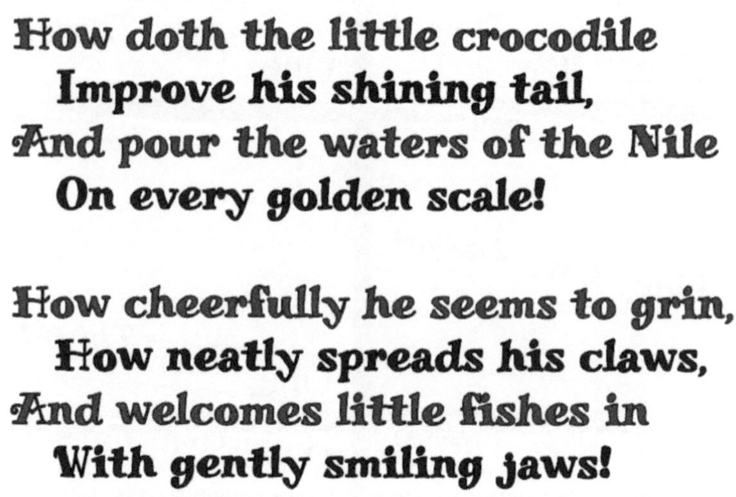

How doth the little crocodile
Improve his shining tail,
And pour the waters of the Nile
On every golden scale!

How cheerfully he seems to grin,
How neatly spreads his claws,
And welcomes little fishes in
With gently smiling jaws!

Figure 4-3. "How doth the little crocodile," set in SVG

themselves. An x attribute establishes a new horizontal starting point, regardless of the previous text position.

Waxing Poetic

Using an absolute x attribute and a relative dy, you can create a line break. The x value is usually set to the same value for each line; it resets the horizontal flow of the text, like a carriage return on an old typewriter. The dy value is equivalent to the desired line height; it shifts the text down like a typewriter's line feed motion.

Example 4-2 uses x and dy to position the lines of a poem (Alice's muddled morality lesson, "How doth the little crocodile," from Lewis Carroll's *Alice in Wonderland*). Each verse is a separate <text> element containing four <tspan> elements for each line. Every second line is inset and styled differently. Figure 4-3 displays the typeset result.

Example 4-2. Typesetting poetry using x, dy, and dx on SVG tspan elements

```
<svg xmlns="http://www.w3.org/2000/svg"
     xml:lang="en-GB" width="4.3in" height="3in">
    <title>How Doth the Little Crocodile - Lewis Carroll</title>
    <desc>From Alice in Wonderland</desc>
    <style>
@import
  url(http://fonts.googleapis.com/css?family=Miltonian+Tattoo);   ❶

        svg {
            font-family: "Miltonian Tattoo", serif;
            font-size: 18pt;
        }
        .verse {
            fill: darkGreen;
            stroke: #031;
            word-spacing: 2px;                                     ❷
        }
        .verse > tspan:nth-child(2n) {                             ❸
            fill: navy;
            stroke: #013;
        }
    </style>
    <rect fill="#CEE" width="100%" height="100%" />
    <text class="verse">                                           ❹
        <tspan dy="1.2em" x="10"
                >How doth the little crocodile</tspan>             ❺
        <tspan dy="1.2em" x="10" dx="1em"
                >Improve his shining tail,</tspan>                 ❻
        <tspan dy="1.2em" x="10"
                >And pour the waters of the Nile</tspan>
        <tspan dy="1.2em" x="10" dx="1em"
                >On every golden scale!</tspan>
    </text>
    <text class="verse" y="50%">                                   ❼
        <tspan dy="1.2em" x="10"
                >How cheerfully he seems to grin,</tspan>
        <tspan dy="1.2em" x="10" dx="1em"
                >How neatly spreads his claws,</tspan>
        <tspan dy="1.2em" x="10"
                >And welcomes little fishes in</tspan>
        <tspan dy="1.2em" x="10" dx="1em"
                >With gently smiling jaws!</tspan>
    </text>
</svg>
```

❶ The SVG uses a decorative web font, Miltonian Tattoo by Pablo Impallari, accessed from Google Font's repository of free typefaces. We'll discuss more about web fonts in Chapter 10.

❷ The letters are stroked, which can make them seem overly close together. A small amount of extra `word-spacing` helps maintain legibility.

❸ An `nth-child(2n)` selector styles every other line differently, in blue instead of green.

❹ There are no positioning attributes on the first `<text>` element: both x and y default to 0.

❺ Each line (`<tspan>`) resets the x position to a left margin of 10px. Each line also shifts the vertical position (`dy`) by 1.2em. For the first line, this offset is measured from the $y=0$ position set by default on the `<text>`.

❻ Every other line has a `dx` attribute, which adds an inset from the margin created by the `x="10"` attribute. Although you could combine the x and dx values, keeping them separate helps clarify the differing purposes, and also allows you to use different units for each.

❼ The second verse follows the same structure, except that it starts from a y position of 50%, halfway down the graphic.

All these attributes might seem a little excessive to create simple line breaks. In a way, it is. SVG was not designed to set paragraphs of text. However, it can be used to set complicated text layouts where the exact position of each text element is important.

Example 4-3 sets another poem from *Alice in Wonderland*: "The Mouse's Tale." In the book, Alice mishears the title as "The Mouse's Tail," and therefore imagines the words arranged in the shape of a long, curvy appendage that gets narrower toward the tip. This is known as a *concrete poem*, where the artistry of the text has as much to do with the way it is printed as the words themselves. Figure 4-4 shows the final typeset text.

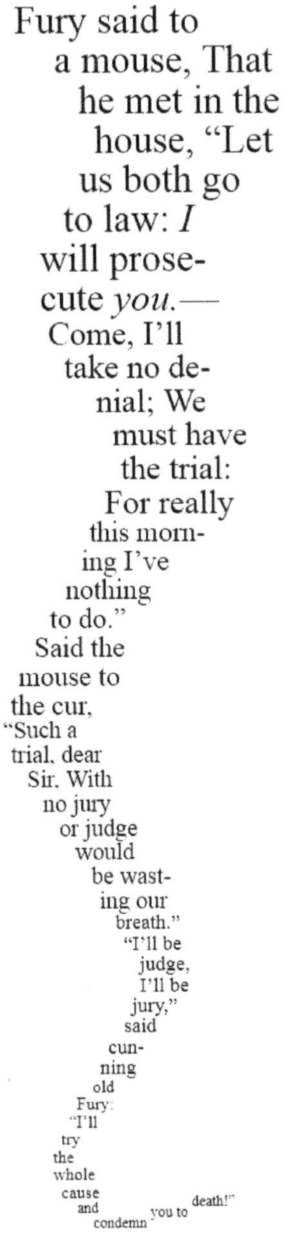

Fury said to
a mouse, That
he met in the
house, "Let
us both go
to law: *I*
will prose-
cute *you*.—
Come, I'll
take no de-
nial; We
must have
the trial:
For really
this morn-
ing I've
nothing
to do."
Said the
mouse to
the cur,
"Such a
trial, dear
Sir. With
no jury
or judge
would
be wast-
ing our
breath."
"I'll be
judge,
I'll be
jury,"
said
cun-
ning
old
Fury:
"I'll
try
the
whole
cause
and   you to   death!"
condemn

Figure 4-4. "The Mouse's Tale," set in SVG

Example 4-3. Typesetting concrete poetry

```
<svg xmlns="http://www.w3.org/2000/svg"
    xml:lang="en-GB" width="100%" height="47.5em">
    <title>The Mouse's Tale - Lewis Carroll</title>
    <desc>From Alice in Wonderland</desc>
    <style>
        svg {
            font-family: serif;
            font-size: medium;
        }
        text {
            font-size: 150%;                    ❶
        }
        .em {
            font-style: italic;                 ❷
        }
        .smaller {
            font-size: 85%;                     ❸
        }
    </style>
    <text>                                       ❹
      <tspan dy="1em" x="50%" dx="-2.68em">Fury said to</tspan>  ❺
      <tspan dy="1em" x="50%" dx="-1.65em">a mouse, That</tspan>
      <tspan dy="1em" x="50%" dx="-1.03em">he met in the</tspan>
      <tspan dy="1em" x="50%" dx="-0.62em">house, "Let</tspan>   ❻
      <tspan dy="1em" x="50%" dx="-1.03em">us both go</tspan>
      <tspan dy="1em" x="50%" dx="-1.44em">to law:
            <tspan class="em">I</tspan></tspan>               ❼
      <tspan dy="1em" x="50%" dx="-2.06em">will prose-</tspan>
      <tspan dy="1em" x="50%" dx="-2.06em">cute
            <tspan class="em">you.</tspan>-</tspan>
      <tspan class="smaller">                                  ❽
        <tspan dy="1em" x="50%" dx="-2.19em">Come, I'll</tspan>
        <tspan dy="1em" x="50%" dx="-1.7em">take no de-</tspan>
        <tspan dy="1em" x="50%" dx="-0.73em">nial; We </tspan>
        <tspan dy="1em" x="50%" dx="-0.24em">must have</tspan>
        <tspan dy="1em" x="50%" dx="-0em">the trial:</tspan>
        <tspan dy="1em" x="50%" dx="-0.49em">For really</tspan>
        <tspan class="smaller">                                ❾
          <tspan dy="1em" x="50%" dx="-1.14em">this morn-</tspan>
          <tspan dy="1em" x="50%" dx="-1.43em">ing I've</tspan>
          <tspan dy="1em" x="50%" dx="-2em">nothing</tspan>
          <tspan dy="1em" x="50%" dx="-2.57em">to do."</tspan>
          <tspan dy="1em" x="50%" dx="-3.14em">Said the</tspan>
          <tspan dy="1em" x="50%" dx="-3.71em">mouse to</tspan>
          <tspan dy="1em" x="50%" dx="-4em">the cur,</tspan>
          <tspan class="smaller">
            <tspan dy="1em" x="50%" dx="-5.04em">"Such a</tspan>
            <tspan dy="1em" x="50%" dx="-4.7em">trial, dear</tspan>
            <tspan dy="1em" x="50%" dx="-4.03em">Sir, With</tspan>
```

```
<tspan dy="1em" x="50%" dx="-3.36em">no jury</tspan>
<tspan dy="1em" x="50%" dx="-2.69em">or judge</tspan>
<tspan dy="1em" x="50%" dx="-2.02em">would</tspan>
<tspan dy="1em" x="50%" dx="-1.34em">be wast-</tspan>
<tspan dy="1em" x="50%" dx="-1.01em">ing our</tspan>
<tspan class="smaller">
    <tspan dy="1em" x="50%" dx="-0.4em">breath."</tspan>
    <tspan dy="1em" x="50%" dx="-0em">"I'll be</tspan>
    <tspan dy="1em" x="50%" dx="0.79em">judge,</tspan>
    <tspan dy="1em" x="50%" dx="0.79em">I'll be</tspan>
    <tspan dy="1em" x="50%" dx="0.4em">jury,"</tspan>
    <tspan dy="1em" x="50%" dx="-0em">said</tspan>
    <tspan dy="1em" x="50%" dx="-0.79em">cun-</tspan>
    <tspan dy="1em" x="50%" dx="-1.19em">ning</tspan>
    <tspan class="smaller">
      <tspan dy="1em" x="50%" dx="-1.86em">old</tspan>
      <tspan dy="1em" x="50%" dx="-2.79em">Fury:</tspan>
      <tspan dy="1em" x="50%" dx="-3.26em">"I'll</tspan>
      <tspan dy="1em" x="50%" dx="-3.72em">try</tspan>
      <tspan dy="1em" x="50%" dx="-4.19em">the</tspan>
      <tspan dy="1em" x="50%" dx="-4.19em">whole</tspan>
      <tspan dy="1em" x="50%" dx="-3.72em">cause</tspan>
      <tspan class="smaller">
        <tspan dy="1em" x="50%" dx="-3.29em">and</tspan>
        <tspan dy="1em" x="50%" dx="-2.19em"
                      >condemn</tspan>                      ❿
        <tspan dy="-0.7em">you to</tspan>
        <tspan dy="-0.7em">death!"</tspan>
      </tspan>
    </tspan>
  </tspan>
      </tspan>
    </tspan>
  </tspan>                                         ⓫
      </tspan>
    </text>
</svg>
```

❶ The text will start out at a font size that is half-again as large as
   the user's normal text. The medium font size is explicitly set on
   the `<svg>` itself to circumvent the font-size error in embedded
   SVG images in WebKit/Blink browsers.

❷ Because SVG does not have an `<em>` element that would by
   default italicize text, emphasized words within the poem are
   styled using a special em class.

❸ As the poem progresses, the font will get smaller and smaller,
   each time set to 85% of the previous value.

❹ Again, the main `<text>` element uses the default position values; the horizontal position will be reset for each line, while the vertical position of the first line is calculated as a one-line offset from the top of the graphic.

❺ Each line is shifted down with `dy="1em"` and is reset horizontally with `x="50%"`. The actual shape of the text is controlled by the `dx` offsets, which were generated by hand—viewing the file and then adjusting the attributes—to create the desired shape.

❻ Unicode characters are used for typographically correct quotation marks and dashes; alternatively, numeric entities could have been used. Since this is an SVG file, HTML named entities such as `&rdquo;` or `&mdash;` are not available.

❼ The italicized spans are simply more `<tspan>` elements, but without any positioning attributes.

❽ The `font-size` change is also created by a `<tspan>` without positioning attributes, but in this case it *contains* all the remaining lines of the poem.

❾ Subsequent `smaller` sections are nested inside the previous, so that the percentage reductions in font size accumulate.

❿ The final curl of the tail is created by *not* resetting the horizontal position between spans, and by reversing the direction of the vertical `dy` adjustment.

⓫ At the end of it all, be sure to close up all your `<tspan>` elements, otherwise all you'll see are XML validation errors!

The use of both x and dx on each line of text may seem excessive, but it allows the entire SVG to adjust to fit any width page and remain centered. Similarly, the use of em units for the height ensures that it will adjust vertically even if the user needs to increase the base font size in order to read the tiny text at the end.

Future Focus
Improved Text Layout Control

SVG may not be designed to set paragraphs of text, but sometimes it would be nice if it could. In diagrams and data visualizations, you don't care so much about the exact position of each word in a label, but you do care if those words run off the edge of the page. And when text is dynamic—or when font size or style is left up to user preferences—it can be difficult to prevent this from happening with explicitly positioned text spans.

SVG 2 will support text that wraps to a new line without explicit intervention by the SVG author. The currently proposed syntax would use a new presentation attribute, `inline-size`, that defines the maximum length of a single line of text. If the normal length of the text flow exceeds it, it would break (at the nearest word boundary) and restart a new line, at the original horizontal position (for horizontal text), offset by the value of the CSS `line-height` property.

When an `inline-size` value is set, additional **dx** and **dy** values would be ignored: You can *either* have full control of layout, or you can have automatically wrapping text, not both.

Another change, however, could make these poetry layouts easier: **x**, **y**, **dx**, and **dy** will *probably* become presentation attributes. As a result, you would be able to remove much of the repetition in the code by using CSS rules to set the position and offset of each line. For example, for the alternating inset lines of Example 4-2 ("How doth the little crocodile"), you could use the following styles:

```
.verse > tspan {
    x: 10px;
    dy: 1.2em;
}
.verse > tspan:nth-child(2n) {
    dx: 1em;
}
```

At the time of writing, the exact syntax for the presentation attributes/CSS properties has not been decided. As we'll see in the next section, the **x** and **y** attributes on text elements can take multiple values, and that is different from the attributes of the same names on other shapes. A style property with a different name might be introduced to keep the two syntaxes separate.

For artistic layouts like the mouse's tail in Example 4-3, work in both SVG and CSS may have a completely different solution. Instead of describing the position of individual lines, you would describe the shape that you wanted the lines of text to fit within, and let the browser wrap the text as required.

A number of the latest browsers already support non-rectangular text wrapping around floated objects in CSS layouts. The effect is created using the **shape-outside** property, defined in the CSS Shapes Module Level 1. The value of this property is either an image file (in which case, the transparency is used to generate the shape) or a CSS Shapes function. SVG would extend this to also allow a reference to an SVG shape within the document.

There would also be a **shape-inside** property that would allow you to define a region into which the browser should fit the lines of text. This option was also initially proposed for CSS Shapes, but was delayed due to the complexity of determining how other aspects of CSS layout would apply inside a shape.

Fitting text within a shape will likely be more straightforward within SVG. At the time of writing, no implementations exist in web browsers, but vector graphics programs can generate the text layout and then convert it to spans of explicitly positioned SVG text.

CHAPTER 5

Off-Kilter Characters

If you want full control over the layout of graphical text, why stop at positioning lines of text? Sometimes, for fun or fussy designs, you'll want to position individual characters.

If you want to style individual letters with CSS, each one needs to be its own element. You might therefore expect that it would be necessary to wrap each character in its own `<tspan>` element in order to position individual letters in SVG. You *could* do this—but you don't have to. The SVG text positioning options allow you to position individual characters within a larger text element.

You're also not restricted to strict horizontal and vertical positions. This chapter introduces the `rotate` attribute for controlling the angle of individual characters.

Multiple Positions

All the text-positioning attributes (x, y, dx, and dy) can take a list of values, which will get assigned character by character to the content.

As with most of SVG, the list of values can be either space-separated or comma-separated.

Any whitespace characters at the start of the text string are normally removed before assigning positions. Spaces in the middle of the text are collapsed, so that any amount of whitespace in the code counts as a single space character for positioning. These behaviors can be changed, as described in "Working with Whitespace" on page 98.

Example 5-1 creates a simple example of this effect, using x and y lists to explicitly position the letters of the word "Wiggle" in an up-and-down wiggled layout. Figure 5-1 shows the result.

Example 5-1. Positioning individual characters within SVG text

```
<svg xmlns="http://www.w3.org/2000/svg"
     xml:lang="en" width="4in" height="1in">
    <title>Positioning Individual Characters</title>
    <style type="text/css">
        svg {
            font: bold italic 0.5in serif;
            fill: royalBlue;
            stroke: navy;
        }
    </style>
    <rect fill="#CEE" stroke="none" width="100%" height="100%" />
    <text x="0      1.0in 1.6in 2.2in 3.0in 3.6in"
          y="0.8in 0.4in 0.8in 0.4in 0.8in 0.4in"
          >Wiggle</text>
</svg>
```

Figure 5-1. Text with custom character positions

Because there are six characters in "Wiggle" and six lengths given in both the x and y attribute lists, each character has its own explicit position. If there were more characters than values, the remaining characters would be positioned relative to the character before them using the normal text layout rules.

When the attribute only contains a single value—as in all the examples from Chapter 4—it is applied to the first character; the rest of the text string is automatically positioned relative to that point.

A similar-but-not-identical layout can be created by instead using a list of values for dx and dy:

```
<text x="0" y="0.8in"
    dx="0  0.5in 0.5in  0.5in 0.5in  0.5in"
    dy="0 -0.4in 0.4in -0.4in 0.4in -0.4in"
    >Wiggle</text>
```

The results are not identical because the dx offsets are *added* to the offset created by the width of the letters themselves. The final position will depend on the font used. In contrast, absolute x values are not affected by the amount of space consumed by the text.

The positioning attributes are independent, and any or none can be specified as lists. If any character does not have positioning values assigned to it, it is positioned as normal beside the previous character in the string.

One use of dx is to mimic the effect of letter-spacing or word-spacing, which are not yet supported for SVG text in Firefox. These properties add a fixed amount of space after every letter or word, respectively; they are particularly useful in SVG to help space out text with thick outlines.

To replace letter-spacing, you need to create a dx attribute with the same value repeated for the length of the text. For word-spacing, you'll need to mix the spacing value with zeros so that only whitespace characters are adjusted. Both the spacing properties and dx can also take negative values to compress the text.

If you're using right-to-left text, you'll have to use negative offset values for positive spacing and vice versa. Chapter 7 discusses more issues with right-to-left text.

Positioning adjustments (and also any non-zero letter-spacing value) should normally turn off the use of optional ligatures (a single glyph to represent multiple adjacent characters) so that all letters are spaced evenly. However, some scripts or fonts have *required* ligatures—certain character sequences are always replaced by a combined glyph—or cursive connections between letters. Changing the spacing between letters in these cases is problematic. Some fonts and rendering software can stretch out cursive connections in a typographically acceptable manner, but others cannot.

Furthermore, many browsers do not correctly select the word-beginning, middle, and word-ending forms of a letter if the entire word is not positioned as a whole.

When using scripts or fonts that have cursive connections or different glyph forms for different positions in a word, be sure to test carefully before using character-by-character positioning.

Conflicting Positions

When you have `<text>` elements with nested `<tspan>` elements, you can specify the character positions on either the parent or child element. Positions specified on a parent element cascade through to characters inside nested `<tspan>` elements.

This means that is possible for two different values to be specified for the same character, if the same attribute is also set on the `<tspan>`. In this case, the value from the inner element replaces the inherited value for that character.

The character-by-character effect of positioning results in a non-intuitive result when using dx and dy on both `<text>` and `<tspan>`. If there are no characters within the `<text>` before the start of the `<tspan>`, the offset on the parent has no effect. The following two text elements result in the exact same position:

```
<text dx="50"><tspan dx="30">content</tspan></text>
<text><tspan dx="30">content</tspan></text>
```

All of the dx values apply to the "c" in "content," and the value on the `<tspan>` overrides the value on the `<text>`. Similarly, positioning values on a `<tspan>` never affect content not included in that span.

This means that attributes on an *empty* `<tspan>` (with no characters) have no effect on the rest of the text, even if they include absolute x or y positions.

Example 5-2 presents a more complicated example of conflicting character position attributes, which combine to create Figure 5-2. The use of conflicting values isn't recommended, if for no other reason than it makes your code confusing to read. But it's included here in case it can help you debug a layout that isn't working the way you intend!

Example 5-2. Positioning individual characters and spans within SVG text

```
<svg xmlns="http://www.w3.org/2000/svg"
    xml:lang="en" width="10cm" height="3.5cm">
    <title>Character and tspan Position adjustments</title>
    <style type="text/css">
        svg {
            font-family: serif;
            font-size: 12mm;
            fill: navy;
        }
        .em {
            fill: royalBlue;
        }
        .strong {
            stroke: navy;
            font-style: italic;
        }
    </style>
    <rect fill="#CEE" width="100%" height="100%" />
    <text x="5mm" y="3cm"
          dy="-30 30 -30 30 -30 30 -30 30 -30 30 -30 30 -30 30"
          >One,
        <tspan class="em" dy="-15" dx="3mm">Two,</tspan>
        <tspan class="strong em" dx="3mm"
               dy="-15 10 10 10 10"
               >Three!</tspan>
    </text>
</svg>
```

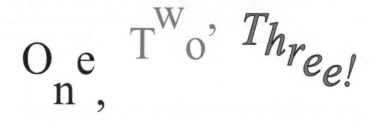

Figure 5-2. Text with custom character positions and styling

To understand how the code in Example 5-2 created the layout in Figure 5-2, it helps to write out the text and offsets, character by character:

text	dy	-30	30	-30	30	-30	30	-30	30	-30	30	-30	30	-30	30	
	char	O	n	e	,	_										
tspan	dy						-15									
	char						T	w	o	,	_					
tspan	dy											-15	10	10	10	10	
	char											T	h	r	e	e	
final	dy	-30	30	-30	30	-30	-15	-30	30	-30	30	-15	10	10	10	10	0
	char	O	n	e	,	_	T	w	o	,	_	T	h	r	e	e	!

The alternating up-and-down dy values set on the <text> apply to individual characters *including the whitespace* (shown as underlines in the table), except where the values are replaced by a value from a <tspan>. For the word "Two," there is a single value, which replaces the offset on the "T," but not the wiggle pattern on the rest of the word. For the word "Three!", all the letters have explicit values from the <tspan>, so the values on the <text> are ignored. However, by the time you reach the exclamation mark (!), the list of values on both elements have been exhausted. It is therefore positioned directly after the previous letter with no offset.

Twisted Letters

If letter-by-letter positioning is not enough for you, you can also specify letter-by-letter rotations. The `rotate` attribute on `<text>` or `<tspan>` accepts a list of numbers that will be treated as rotational angles in degrees. Each individual character is rotated fron the baseline by that amount.

As usual in SVG, positive rotations are clockwise and negative rotations are counterclockwise.

The angles in `rotate` are not cumulative: each angle is measured relative to the baseline.

Just as an x, y, dx, or dy value affects all the letters that come after it until the position is reset, so a `rotate` value affects all the characters until reset. If you give a single value to `rotate`, it applies to all the characters in that element. *Unlike* the positioning values, however, the rotation setting persists even if an intervening `<tspan>` set a different rotational value for a section of the text.

Example 5-3 uses the `rotate` attribute on both `<text>` and `<tspan>` elements, with the result shown in Figure 5-3.

Example 5-3. Rotating individual characters within SVG text

```
<svg xmlns="http://www.w3.org/2000/svg"
    xml:lang="en" width="4in" height="0.7in">
    <title>Rotating Individual Characters</title>
    <style type="text/css">
        svg {
            font: bold italic 0.5in serif;
            fill: royalBlue;
            stroke: navy;
        }
    </style>
    <rect fill="#CEE" stroke="none" width="100%" height="100%" />
    <text x="0.2in" y="0.5in" rotate="-45 0 15 -15 15"
        >Jiggle
        <tspan rotate="-25">giggle</tspan>
        jig!
    </text>
</svg>
```

Figure 5-3. Text with rotated characters

An important thing to note in Figure 5-3 is that the rotations do not affect the normal text offsets between characters along the baseline. As a result, the letters end up overlapping or spaced apart, depending on whether they are rotating closer to or farther away from each other.

The origin of rotation is the current *text position* point: the point created by the x, y, dx, and dy attributes as well as any offsets from previous letters. For the examples so far, that has been the point where the left side of the letter intersects the baseline of the text.

 The origin of rotation will be affected by the text direction and the text-anchor property (which we'll discuss in Chapter 6).

So what is all this character-by-character layout used for? Not for setting lines of text, which are best left to the browser's default typesetting algorithms. This is for text as a graphic, when you want as much control over the letters as over the rest of your image.

Example 5-4 creates some comic-book exclamations using positioned text. The example also emphasizes the difference between a transform rotation—which changes the position of the baseline and the direction of *x* and *y* offsets—versus character-by-character rotations, which do not affect the axes. The result is shown in Figure 5-4.

Example 5-4. Using multiple attributes for precisely positioned text

```
<svg xmlns="http://www.w3.org/2000/svg"
     xmlns:xlink="http://www.w3.org/1999/xlink"
     xml:lang="en"
     width="400px" height="400px" viewBox="0 0 400 400">
  <title>Explosive Text</title>
```

Figure 5-4. Explosive comic book text

```
<style type="text/css">
    .dynamic-lettering {
        font-family: "Gill Sans Ultra Bold",
                     "Gill Sans", "Gill Sans MT",
                     "Showcard Gothic",
                     "Cooper Black", "Cooper",
                     "Arial Black", "Arial",
                     "Impact", sans-serif;          ❶
        font-size: 100px;
        font-weight: 900;                           ❷
        fill: url(#yellow-red) orangeRed;
        stroke: url(#red-brown) red;
        stroke-width: 3px;
    }

</style>
<defs>
    <linearGradient id="yellow-red"
```

```
                        gradientTransform="rotate(90)">
            <stop stop-color="yellow" offset="0"/>
            <stop stop-color="red" offset="0.8"/>
            <stop stop-color="maroon" offset="1.0"/>          ❸
        </linearGradient>
        <linearGradient id="red-brown"
                        gradientTransform="rotate(90)" >
            <stop stop-color="orangeRed" offset="0"/>
            <stop stop-color="maroon" offset="1.0"/>
        </linearGradient>
    </defs>
    <rect height="100%" width="100%" fill="aquamarine"/>
    <g class="dynamic-lettering">
        <text transform="translate(40,165) rotate(-15)"
              dy="0 20 -30 20"
              >BAM!</text>                                    ❹
        <text x="75" y="375"
              dx="0    -70  -30   8 -25"
              dy="0    -70  -80  50  45"
        rotate="-70 -15   35  10  30">BOOM!</text>            ❺
    </g>
</svg>
```

❶ A list of heavyweight, mostly sans-serif, fonts are provided as options.

❷ If available, the heaviest bold variant of the font will be used.

❸ The text is filled and stroked with linear gradients that are each oriented at a 90° rotation from default—in other words, from top to bottom.

❹ The first text element ("BAM!") is positioned and rotated using a transformation. A dy attribute then shifts the characters up and down, relative to the rotated baseline.

❺ The second ("BOOM!") text element is positioned using x and y, and then individual characters are rotated and offset vertically and horizontally using dx, dy, and rotate.

The character positions affect the gradients used in Example 5-4. In Chapter 3, we noted how gradients stretch to fit the bounding box of the entire <text> element, even if the gradient is only used on a <tspan>. That issue isn't relevant here: there are two different <text> elements, so each one has its own gradient from gold to red.

Figure 5-5. Comparing gradient filled rotated text in Firefox 38 (left) and Internet Explorer 11 (right)

However, the bounding box *is* affected by the shifts in position of individual characters.

The SVG 1.1 specifications imply, but don't explicitly say, that the bounding box of a `<text>` element should also include the individual character rotations applied with `rotate`. However, most browsers treat character rotations the same way they treat transformations: as a rotation of the entire coordinate system, including paint server content.

 All browsers with the exception of Firefox will rotate gradient and pattern fills on individual rotated characters.

To demonstrate the difference between browsers, Figure 5-5 repeats Figure 5-4, which is a screenshot from Firefox, comparing it side by side with the same SVG as rendered by Internet Explorer 11.

The first word ("BAM!") looks the same, because all browsers rotate the gradient when the `<text>` element itself is transformed. However, the second word ("BOOM!") looks uneven—with high contrast between letters—in Internet Explorer (and also Blink and WebKit browsers, which use the same painting strategy). The positions of the letters on the page, after character rotation, does not match their position used to calculate the gradient. The gradients are still affected by the dy and dx offsets, however, so the colors are not the same in each letter.

The gradients aren't the only aspect of the SVG that differ from browser to browser. Even on the author's own computer, not all browsers are able to access the "Gill Sans Ultra Bold" system font, despite the many variations on the name given. On another computer, this font might not even be available. In Chapter 10, we'll revisit this example to examine the effects of fonts on layout.

We've now covered positioning text elements, positioning text spans, and positioning individual characters. In each case, the position you specify has been the *start* of a section of text. In Chapter 6, we explore how to position text centered over, or ending at, a point.

Future Focus
Transformed Text Spans

As Example 5-4 demonstrated, the `transform` attribute applies to `<text>` elements. In contrast, in SVG 1.1, you cannot transform individual `<tspan>` segments, which are not shapes drawn to the page on their own. That caused confusion, and SVG 2 will allow spans to be transformed, with an attribute or with the CSS 3 `transform` property.

The `rotate` attribute, like **x**, **y**, **dx**, and **dy**, will probably become a presentation attribute. As mentioned in the previous section, there has been some hesitation about committing to this change because `<text>` and `<tspan>` elements are the only place where lists of values can be used for an attribute named **x** or **y**.

One other change that has been proposed (but not decided) is the introduction of a syntax to concisely declare a repeating pattern of offsets or rotations, instead of having to list values for each individual character.

CHAPTER 6

Casting Anchor

Every modern word processor has the option to left-align, right-align, center, or justify text. CSS text layout uses the `text-align` property to choose between these options for positioning text within the layout box.

For CSS or word processors, the page layout defines margins on either side of the text region. Alignment settings determine how extra whitespace is shifted within this space: accumulating on one side or the other, divided evenly on either side, or distributed in between words.

In SVG, there are no margins and no boxes. Each line of text is just as long as it needs to be. As we have seen, it might not even be a straight line. SVG *does* provide tools to center or right-align text. The options, however, are not as straightforward as the `text-align` property.

Start, Middle, or End

SVG text alignment is controlled by the `text-anchor` property. The point you specify with x and y is the *anchor point* for that span of text, and `text-anchor` controls whether this point is positioned at the start, middle, or end of the span.

The default for `text-anchor` is start. Other values (end or middle) can be specified as a presentation attribute or via CSS.

The `text-anchor` property is inherited, so it can be set once for the entire SVG if desired.

Example 6-1 displays three strings, with the same horizontal position but different `text-anchor` values; Figure 6-1 shows the result. A vertical guideline marks the *x* position used to anchor all the text elements.

Example 6-1. Aligning SVG text around an anchor point

```svg
<svg xmlns="http://www.w3.org/2000/svg"
    xmlns:xlink="http://www.w3.org/1999/xlink"
    xml:lang="en"
    width="4.3in" height="1.72in" viewBox="0 0 400 160">
    <title>Anchoring SVG Text</title>
    <style type="text/css">
        svg {
            font: bold 50px serif;
        }
    </style>
    <rect fill="#CEE" width="100%" height="100%" />
    <line stroke="gray" x1="50%" x2="50%" y2="100%" />

    <text text-anchor="start" fill="darkGreen"
        x="50%" y="1em" >Start</text>
    <text text-anchor="middle" fill="navy"
        x="50%" y="2em" >Middle</text>
    <text text-anchor="end" fill="darkRed"
        x="50%" y="3em" >End</text>
</svg>
```

Start
Middle
End

Figure 6-1. SVG text anchor options

For left-to-right English text like this, start-anchored text ends up on the right of the anchor point (left-aligned to the guideline), middle-anchored text is centered over the anchor, and end-anchored text is positioned on the left of the anchor point (right-aligned relative to the guideline).

Aligning a single line of text like this is straightforward and predictable. But how do you align text that has a mixture of repositioned spans and characters? The answer is that you break it up into *text chunks*.

Text Chunks

For SVG text layout, a text chunk (yes, that is the technical term from the specifications!) is a sequence of characters anchored on an absolutely positioned point. Because we are, so far, dealing with horizontal alignment of horizontal text, only the absolute x values matter. Changes in y position won't affect the horizontal alignment.

The text chunks used for alignment purposes can span multiple <tspan> elements, or they can be individual characters.

Any character that is assigned an absolute position in the text's inline direction becomes the start of a new chunk.

Example 6-2 presents text in which some, but not all, characters have explicit x values. The text—and a guideline that shows the anchor position—is duplicated with a <use> element that resets both the fill color and the text-anchor property. As an inherited style property, text-anchor can be changed when text is reused (assuming the original text used an inherited or default value).

Duplicated text should only be used for graphical effects, such as reflections or shadows. It is not recognized as text by assistive technologies such as screen readers.

Figure 6-2 shows the result.

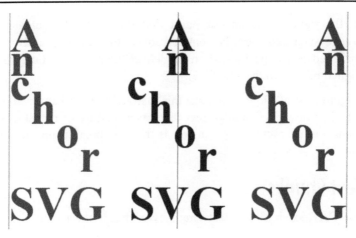

Figure 6-2. SVG text anchor effects on complex text layout

Example 6-2. Aligning SVG text with character and span positioning

```
<svg xmlns="http://www.w3.org/2000/svg"
    xmlns:xlink="http://www.w3.org/1999/xlink"
    xml:lang="en"
    width="4.3in" height="2.4in" viewBox="0 0 400 225">
    <title>Anchoring Custom-Positioned Text</title>
    <style type="text/css">
        svg {
            font: bold 50px serif;
        }
    </style>
    <rect fill="#CEE" width="100%" height="100%" />

    <g text-anchor="start"
        fill="darkGreen" transform="translate(20,0)">         ❶
        <g id="sample">                                        ❷
            <line stroke="gray" y2="100%" />                   ❸
            <text x="0 0 0" y="40"
                dy="0 25 25 25 25 25"
                >Anchor                                        ❹
                <tspan x="0" dy="1em">SVG</tspan></text>       ❺
        </g>
    </g>
    <use xlink:href="#sample" text-anchor="middle"
        fill="navy" transform="translate(200,0)" />           ❻
    <use xlink:href="#sample" text-anchor="end"
        fill="darkRed" transform="translate(380,0)" />
</svg>
```

❶ The first block of text uses `start` alignment and dark green fill; these styles are set on a wrapping `<g>` element so they won't be copied when the text is duplicated.

❷ An inner `<g>` element groups together the text and the guideline; this group has an `id` value and will be duplicated by the `<use>` elements.

❸ The `<line>` has a single attribute, y2; the others all default to 0. The guideline will therefore be drawn along the *y*-axis (*x*=0) in the transformed coordinate system.

❹ Every character in the first word is given its own vertical position with dy; the first three characters have their horizontal position reset to *x*=0.

❺ The second word is its own `<tspan>`, with a single x value.

❻ The `<use>` elements copy the inner group with the guideline and text, but translate the *x*=0 line to the right so the samples don't overlap. The `<use>` elements also specify the `text-anchor` and `fill` properties as presentation attributes.

Because of the mix of character and span positioning, the text chunks are "A", "n", "chor", and "SVG". The alignment for the single letters is straightforward and works as expected. Each letter-chunk is aligned against or centered over the guideline. For the larger chunks, even though the *first* character in the chunk has the position value, it is the chunk as a whole that is horizontally aligned.

The chunk as a whole includes the space after the word "Anchor," which gets added to the diagonal letters. This pushes the "r" away from the end guideline, and unbalances the centered text.

 When aligning a horizontal text chunk around an anchor point, the *entire* horizontal offset for that chunk is aligned, including any whitespace, `letter-spacing`, `word-spacing`, or dx offsets on characters other than the first one.

A dx offset on the first character in the chunk—the character that has the x anchor value—does not add to the length of text being centered or aligned. Instead, it shifts the anchor point. Whether it moves the text away from the x anchor point, or pulls the text over top of it, will depend on which part of the text chunk (start or end) is being anchored and which direction the text is written in. An offset on the anchor point is always measured in the coordinate system: negative offsets move left and positive offsets move right.

Future Focus
Alignment in Multiline SVG

The introduction of automatically wrapping text in SVG 2 requires additional alignment options. The CSS **text-align** property will be adopted to control alignment of text within shapes. At the time of writing, other details—such as how **text-align** will interact with **text-anchor** to position lines of text limited by **inline-size**—have not been decided.

Working with Whitespace

The inclusion of starting and ending whitespace within the aligned text chunk is a frequent source of frustration in SVG text layout. There are a number of workarounds you can use:

- Remove all whitespace at the start and end of the text content, so that the opening and closing < and > markup characters are immediately adjacent to the words.

  This is not recommended for multiple <tspan> elements within a single <text> element. It ruins the text for accessibility purposes—or for copy-and-paste selections—jamming all the letters together into a single word, regardless of their appearance on the screen.

- Ensure that the whitespace is always at the side of the text chunk where it won't affect alignment. For start anchors, put the whitespace at the end of the chunk. For end anchors, put it at the start. For middle, add whitespace at both ends.

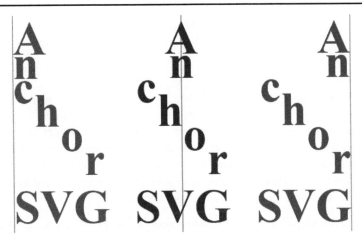

Figure 6-3. SVG text anchor effects on complex text layout, when the whitespace is a separate "chunk"

This has been used throughout the book in the examples with multiple `<tspan>` lines. However, it means that you cannot later change the alignment without editing the text.

- Create a separate text chunk to contain the whitespace—which is absolutely positioned in the *x* direction but doesn't affect the *y*-position—by inserting the whitespace at the start of the `<tspan>` and using an extra value at the start of each positioning attribute list:

```
<text x="0 0 0" y="40"
      dy="0 25 25 25 25 25"
      >Anchor<tspan
      x="0 0" dy="0 1em"> SVG</tspan></text>
```

This strategy is the most robust, preserving the layout *and* the word breaks if you later change the alignment, as shown in Figure 6-3.

None of these options are ideal. The layout is improved in Figure 6-3, but at the cost of rather confusing markup.

In contrast, whitespace at the very start or end of a `<text>` element is ignored. It does not affect layout or the assignment of character-by-character positioning attributes.

Internet Explorer does not ignore whitespace at the end of the text string. For consistent alignment, always place the closing `</text>` tag immediately after the last character.

The previous discussion describes "whitespace" as a single, amorphous entity. For the most part, that's how it works in SVG. Any number of consecutive space, tab, or newline characters in your SVG code gets collapsed into a single space character when the text is inserted into the SVG graphic. Other blank characters, such as the non-breaking space, do not collapse. This whitespace collapsing works the same as the default behavior for HTML.

Rarely, you will want to include multiple spaces. SVG 1.1 uses the `xml:space` attribute for this purpose. The default behavior is equivalent to `xml:space="default"`. Setting a value of `preserve` will prevent the collapsing of multiple whitespace characters, or the trimming of spaces at the start and end of the string.

 Internet Explorer and WebKit do not currently support `xml:space="preserve"`. Firefox supports `xml:space` on any element, with the effect applied to all child content. Blink browsers only support `xml:space` when directly applied to a text-containing element.

For the most part, `xml:space="preserve"` isn't recommended when writing your own code: you can get better control of the SVG layout using `dx` to add extra space between characters. However, many graphics programs use preserved spaces to implement What-You-See-Is-What-You-Get (WYSIWYG) behavior. Designers working with a visual editor expect to be able to type spaces in the text and have them reflected in the graphic.

 You don't need to declare a namespace prefix for `xml:space`; the `xml` prefix is reserved in all XML documents, including SVG.

If you do use xml:space, be aware that it only preserves whitespace as *spaces*: each tab or line break is transformed into a space character.

Future Focus
Whitespace Control in SVG 2

SVG 2 will adopt the CSS **white-space** property for controlling whitespace, deprecating the use of the **xml:space** attribute. It takes one of five values, determining whether whitespace is collapsed, whether line breaks in the code are preserved, and whether automatic line breaks are inserted:

normal
> Collapse whitespace and line breaks; allow automatic line breaks

pre
> Preserve whitespace and line breaks; do not insert automatic line breaks

nowrap
> Collapse whitespace and line breaks; do not insert automatic line breaks (essentially, the default SVG 1.1 behavior)

pre-wrap
> Preserve whitespace and line breaks; allow automatic line breaks

pre-line
> Preserve line breaks, but collapse all other whitespace; allow automatic line breaks

For SVG, any *preserved* line breaks will have a similar effect to automatic line breaks inserted because of **inline-size**: the horizontal position will be reset and the vertical position will be offset by the value of the CSS **line-height** property. Any preserved tab characters will be affected by the CSS **tab-size** property. However, it has not been decided how tab stops will be aligned: relative to the text anchor, or relative to the coordinate system?

If the CSS **white-space** property is set on an element—as a style rule or a presentation attribute—the XML attribute will be ignored. However, the CSS specifications will introduce another **white-space** option that reflects **xml:space="preserve"** to make it easier for implementations to transition to the new rules.

The use of **normal** CSS **white-space** rules will affect the problem with trailing whitespace and text anchors. In CSS, lines are always trimmed of non-preserved whitespace at the begining and end before being aligned in a box. Unfortunately, changing the existing SVG behavior to match CSS may upset existing SVG layouts that have been carefully positioned based on the current rules.

CHAPTER 7

Anchoring in International Waters

Think you've got a handle on SVG text alignment now? Not *too* complicated, is it? (Is it?) Maybe you're wondering, though, why the text-anchor keywords are not simply left, center, and right. It's a good question, and the start of a whole other level of complication.

The examples in the book so far have used English text, laid out left to right the way English text normally is. However, other languages arrange text right to left or top to bottom. Even within English and other Western languages, you may want to use vertical text to fit within the layout of a chart or diagram, or for artistic effect.

SVG includes a number of features to support alternative text modes, and this chapter and the next explain how they are supposed to work. However, some of the features were not well designed, and most are not well implemented in web browsers at the time of writing. These chapters therefore contain many warnings about browser incompatibilities. Where practical, they also offer suggestions for workarounds.

If you are developing designs that use non-Western languages, you will want to test your code thoroughly in any software you need to support.

You can also get involved to make things better in the future: provide feedback on web standards in development, and file bug reports and feature requests with browsers. Many developers involved in SVG and CSS have limited experience with non-

European languages. Even if all you can do is provide practical use cases of how text layout *should* work, it will make a difference.

Starting from the Other End

The start and end values for text-anchor were intended to support mixed-language content without any bias toward left-to-right scripts. It was well-intended, but had the opposite effect: it makes changing the language of SVG designs *more* difficult, not less.

In CSS layout, text is contained by the layout box, and alignment moves text within it. Using start and end values therefore allows the text to align according to the norm for the text language without throwing off the overall layout. In theory, anyway. Unfortunately, these values are still rarely used for text-align on the Web because of a lack of support from Internet Explorer.

In SVG layout, text is aligned relative to a point, not a box. Look through all the examples in previous chapters, and imagine what would happen if the text started from the same anchor point, and then progressed from right to left (or top to bottom) instead of left to right. The text would either overlap graphics or run off the edge of the SVG.

If you're switching between left-to-right and right-to-left languages, you'll often want to use the CSS direction property to specify which direction should be used for layout: ltr or rtl. This will not reverse the characters; the browser will still arrange sequences of characters according to their natural direction as defined in the Unicode specification. However, those sequences of characters will be embedded within an SVG text layout in the direction you specify.

 The default value of the direction property is ltr. It is inherited, and can be used as a presentation attribute in SVG.

Whenever possible, design your layout using the natural direction of the text language you will be using. Many characters, such as punctuation, don't have an implicit direction. They will therefore follow the imposed direction value instead of the native direction of the rest of the text. The text within each layout chunk will be broken into sequences of characters with the same direction, and then those sequences arranged according to the direction property. With direction: ltr, starting punctuation will always be positioned on the left and ending punctuation will be set on the right of the text, even if the remaining text consists entirely of characters ordered from right to left. Punctuation in the middle of the text may match surrounding characters, or may break up the layout completely, depending on how the character is tagged in Unicode.

 When mixing content with different directions, Internet Explorer does not implement the Unicode bidirectional algorithm correctly for SVG. Text sequences can end up in seemingly random positions, offset in the wrong direction from the rest.

If you are translating the text within an SVG diagram, you will need to reverse all the text-anchor values for languages with the reverse text direction in order to keep the text in the same region of the graphic.

To demonstrate the interaction between text-anchor, direction, and the natural direction of text, Example 7-1 uses a script to generate various combinations. It creates SVGs embedded in an HTML table, with English, Arabic, Greek, and Hebrew text aligned start, middle, or end, and either left-to-right or right-to-left direction imposed. Figure 7-1 displays the resulting web page. Note that the order of letters remains the same regardless of the layout direction, but the position of the exclamation mark moves so it is always at the "end" of the text, based on the direction property. The comma in the English text, in contrast, is surrounded by left-to-right characters, and matches it accordingly.

Example 7-1. Using text-anchor and direction on text with different natural directions

```
<!DOCTYPE html>
<html>
<head>
    <meta charset="utf-8"/>
    <title>Multilingual SVG Text Direction and Layout</title>
    <style>
        table {
            width: 100%;
```

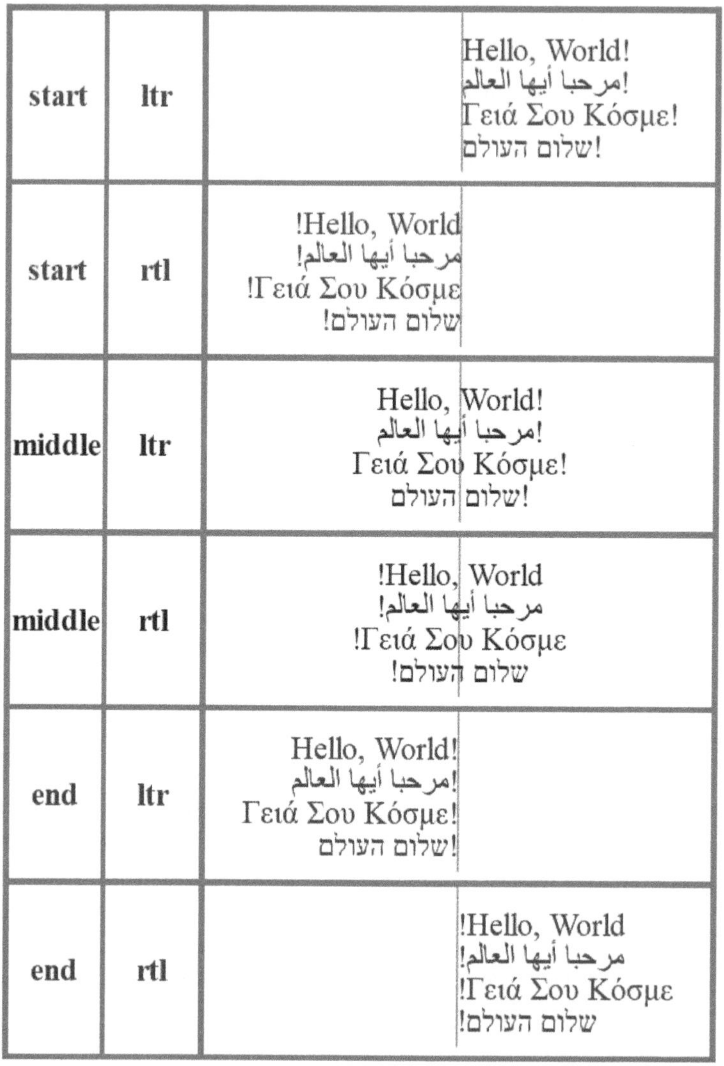

start	**ltr**		Hello, World! مرحبا أيها العالم! Γειά Σου Κόσμε! שלום העולם!
start	**rtl**	!Hello, World مرحبا أيها العالم! !Γειά Σου Κόσμε שלום העולם!	
middle	**ltr**	Hello, World! مرحبا أيها العالم! Γειά Σου Κόσμε! שלום העולם!	
middle	**rtl**	!Hello, World مرحبا أيها العالم! !Γειά Σου Κόσμε שלום העולם!	
end	**ltr**	Hello, World! مرحبا أيها العالم! Γειά Σου Κόσμε! שלום העולם!	
end	**rtl**		!Hello, World مرحبا أيها العالم! !Γειά Σου Κόσμε שלום העולם!

Figure 7-1. SVG text anchor effects with text of different natural and imposed directions

```css
    table-layout: fixed;
    border-collapse: collapse;
}
th:nth-child(n-2) {
    width: 3em;
```

```
        }
        td, th {
            border: solid royalBlue;
            padding: 0;
            background: #DEF;
        }
        svg {
            height: 5em;
            width: 100%;
        }
        line {
            stroke: gray;
        }
        text {
            fill: currentColor;
        }
        .start  { color: darkGreen; }
        .middle { color: navy; }
        .end    { color: darkRed; }
    </style>
</head>
<body>
<script>
(function(){
    var svgNS = "http://www.w3.org/2000/svg";
    var doc = document;

    var strings = [ "Hello, World!",
                    "مرحبا أيها العالم!",
                    "Γειά Σου Κόσμε!",
                    "שלום העולם!" ],
        directions = [ "ltr", "rtl" ],
        anchors = [ "start", "middle", "end" ];

    var table = doc.createElement("table"),
        tbody = doc.createElement("tbody");
    table.insertBefore(tbody, null);

    var row, rowh, rowsub, cell, svg, line, text;
    for (var i=0, a=anchors.length; i<a; i++){
        for (var j=0, d=directions.length; j<d; j++) {
            row = doc.createElement("tr");
            rowh = doc.createElement("th");
            rowh.textContent = anchors[i];
            row.setAttribute("class", anchors[i]);
            row.insertBefore(rowh, null);
            rowsub = doc.createElement("th");
            rowsub.textContent = directions[j];
            row.insertBefore(rowsub, null);

            cell = doc.createElement("td");
```

```
            row.insertBefore(cell, null);

            svg = doc.createElementNS(svgNS, "svg");
            svg.setAttribute("direction", directions[j]);
            svg.setAttribute("text-anchor", anchors[i]);
            cell.insertBefore(svg, null);

            line = doc.createElementNS(svgNS, "line");
            line.setAttribute("x1", "50%");
            line.setAttribute("x2", "50%");
            line.setAttribute("y2", "100%");
            svg.insertBefore(line, null);

            for (var k=0, s=strings.length; k<s; k++) {
                text = doc.createElementNS(svgNS, "text");
                text.textContent = strings[k];
                text.setAttribute("x", "50%");
                text.setAttribute("y", (k+1.5) + "em");
                svg.insertBefore(text, null);
            }
            tbody.insertBefore(row, null);
        }
    }
    doc.body.insertBefore(table, null);
})();
</script>
</body>
</html>
```

For mixed direction text, character-by-character positioning attributes are assigned based on the logical reading order, not the displayed order. Absolutely positioned characters still form new text chunks.

The Unicode bidirectionality rules do not reorder characters between different absolutely positioned text chunks.

Rarely, you want to force characters to be arranged in a specific order regardless of the script's normal direction. This is achieved using the CSS unicode-bidi property, set to a value of bidi-override. This tells the browser to ignore the bidirectional text algorithm defined by Unicode, and lay out the characters in the exact order and direction specified.

In HTML, text direction is controlled by the dir attribute and the <bdo> (bidirectional override) element. To maintain correct language layout in the absence of CSS styling, authors are advised to use these features instead of the CSS direction and unicode-bidi properties.

 When SVG is inline in HTML, Firefox, WebKit, and Blink browsers use the HTML document's direction as the default SVG direction, but Internet Explorer does not. For consistent results, explicitly set direction and unicode-bidi on your SVG elements.

As mentioned in Chapter 5, the direction of the text does not affect the direction of a dx offset. Positive or negative dx values shift the text position toward the positive or negative x-axis, respectively. For right-to-left text, a positive dx will reduce spacing and a negative offset will increase it.

Head to Toe Layout

SVG was also designed to support vertically oriented text. Although the primary purpose was to support languages in which text is naturally written top to bottom, it can also be used for graphical effect, such as to create vertical labels on a chart.

The SVG vertical writing properties currently have limited support. Better support is expected for a new CSS Writing Modes Module. However, the syntax is different—simplifying many of the most confusing aspects of the SVG specification, but adding compatibility headaches.

Firefox never implemented SVG vertical writing. Developers have begun implementing the new CSS vertical writing mode specification, but at the time of writing the user must specifically enable support.

Other browsers' implementations are inconsistent and buggy, especially when mixing right-to-left text direction with vertical writing mode. Blink has the most complete SVG vertical writing implementation, but in versions prior to Chromium 44, the layout is thrown off when the user zooms the browser window.

If using vertical writing in SVG, test your work thoroughly in all browsers and devices you need to support.

For most languages and scripts where vertical writing is common, the character glyphs are positioned upright, one under the other. For other scripts, the entire string of glyphs is rotated sideways. When Latin letters (or Greek or Cyrillic, etc.) are included in upright vertical text, they may likewise be oriented upright or they may be rotated. Cursive scripts such as Arabic would nearly always be rotated sideways when embedded in vertical text, because positioning letters upright one under the other would interrupt the normal word forms of the letters.

A set of related style properties define which of these modes should be used. The `writing-mode` style property defines whether vertical or horizontal text should be used. The SVG 1.1 specifications define many possible values, but they all add up to two different modes:

- `lr`, `lr-tb`, `rl`, or `rl-tb` create horizontal text. The distinction between the `rl` values (right-to-left) and `lr` values (left-to-right) does not have an effect; use the `direction` property for that.

- `tb` or `tb-rl` create vertical text. The `rl` part of the long form indicates that lines are normally stacked from the right to the left across the page; because SVG 1.1 does not have any automatic line wrapping, this is not usually relevant.

These redundant values will be simplified by CSS writing modes, as described later in the chapter. For best support, you will need to use old and new values as fallbacks.

In SVG 1.1, the orientation of the individual characters within vertical text is controlled by the `glyph-orientation-vertical` property. The default value (`auto`) prints characters upright if they come from a script where that is normal, or rotates them otherwise. The upright characters include some special punctuation characters designed for vertical scripts, or variants on Latin characters or numbers that are particularly encoded for display as full-width characters.

To change the `auto` setting, you can set `glyph-orientation-vertical` to an orientation angle that should apply to all characters. The only option that produces logical text is `0`, which forces all the characters to remain upright while stacked top to bottom.

The `glyph-orientation-vertical` can also be set to `90`, `180`, or `270` to rotate characters. However, the results are not particularly readable, and there are no direct equivalents in the new CSS `text-orientation` property in CSS Writing Modes.

If you're looking to create an off-kilter layout with upside-down text, you have more flexibility using `rotate`.

There is also a `glyph-orientation-horizontal` property; it does not include an `auto` value, and the default is an angle of 0 (upright characters).

The glyph orientation settings are only supported in WebKit/Blink browsers. Although Internet Explorer supports the tb writing mode, the glyph orientation is always `auto`.

Example 7-2 demonstrates the use of `writing-mode` and `glyph-orientation-vertical` for mixed Chinese-and-English text and for all-English text. Figure 7-2 shows the result in a browser that supports both features (Chrome). The text is shown with both `start`

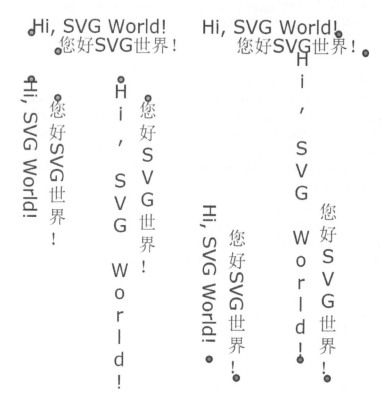

Figure 7-2. Vertical SVG text with various text-anchor and glyph orientation options

and end text anchors, and the anchor point for each text element is marked by a circle.

Example 7-2. Using vertical writing mode in SVG

```
<svg xmlns="http://www.w3.org/2000/svg"
    xmlns:xlink="http://www.w3.org/1999/xlink"
    width="4.3in" height="4.5in">
    <title>Mixed Scripts and Writing Modes</title>
    <style type="text/css">
        svg {
            font: 20px sans-serif;
            stroke-width: 2px;
        }
```

```
    text {
        fill: currentColor;
    }
</style>
<defs>
    <circle id="anchor" r="3px" fill="currentColor"
            stroke="currentColor" fill-opacity="0.5"/>          ❶
</defs>
<rect fill="#CEE" width="100%" height="100%" />
<g color="darkGreen" text-anchor="start">
    <g id="sample" fill="currentColor" >
        <use xlink:href="#anchor" x="1em" y="2em" />
        <text x="1em" y="2em" >Hi, SVG World!</text>         ❷

        <use xlink:href="#anchor" x="2.5em" y="3em" />
        <text x="2.5em" y="3em" >您好 SVG 世界！</text>         ❸
    </g>
    <use xlink:href="#sample" transform="translate(0,50)"
        writing-mode="tb" />                                  ❹
    <use xlink:href="#sample" transform="translate(100,50)"
        writing-mode="tb" glyph-orientation-vertical="0"/> ❺
</g>
<g color="darkRed" text-anchor="end"
    transform="translate(200,0)" >                            ❻
    <use xlink:href="#sample" transform="translate(140,0)" />
    <use xlink:href="#sample" transform="translate(0,350)"
        writing-mode="tb" />
    <use xlink:href="#sample" transform="translate(100,350)"
        writing-mode="tb" glyph-orientation-vertical="0"/>
</g>

</svg>
```

❶ The anchor circle is defined to be centered around the origin, so it will end up centered on whichever (*x,y*) point is defined in the <use> element. It uses the currentColor keyword to set both fill and stroke to the same color, but with different opacity values.

❷ The phrase "Hi, SVG World!" is used as a sample of Latin text.

❸ For comparison with a language with a natural vertical writing mode, the phrase has been translated into traditional Chinese characters; the acronym "SVG" remains written in Latin characters. The exclamation mark at the end is a special Unicode full-width punctuation character which will not normally rotate when typeset vertically. The two text elements have different anchors in both the *x*- and *y*-directions, so they will not overlap regardless of whether they are set horizontally or vertically.

❹ The group containing both text elements and their anchor-markers is duplicated, but with `writing-mode` set to top to bottom (`tb`). The glyph orientation will use the default `auto` setting.

❺ The text and anchors are duplicated again, with top-to-bottom mode but also an explicit upright glyph orientation for all characters.

❻ Finally, all the options are repeated again, but with `text-anchor` set to `end`. The translations have been adjusted to position the anchor points at the far edge of the graphic, so that the text does not overlap or run off the edge.

Once again, all the text direction options do not change the direction of x, y, dx, or dy offsets. Even if top-to-bottom Latin text *looks* the same as text that has been rotated with a transformation, the coordinate system has not changed. Absolute y positions create text chunks for alignment purposes in vertical text, not absolute x positions.

Future Focus

Standardizing Vertical Text Properties for All Web Content

The CSS Writing Modes Level 3 module adopted the idea of writing-mode and glyph orientation from SVG—and then changed the syntax completely. Most of the values from SVG are officially deprecated under the new specification, and should never be used in non-SVG documents.

To create future-proof documents with optimal browser support, use the modern CSS syntax with the SVG 1.1 syntax as a fallback. At the time of writing, the CSS syntax is still treated as experimental in most browsers, requiring either prefixed property names or opt-in user settings. What implementations that do exist may be buggy—but those bugs are being progressively squashed, so by the time you read this the situation may be better.

The main difference in CSS is that **writing-mode** has been made completely independent from **direction**. The **writing-mode** value is now the same for left-to-right and right-to-left horizontal scripts. It controls how lines and blocks

---

are laid out on the page, but not the position of characters within the line. The new values are as follows:

`horizontal-tb`
Lines flow horizontally; new lines appear below previous lines

`vertical-rl`
Lines flow vertically; new lines appear to the left of previous lines

`vertical-lr`
Lines flow vertically; new lines appear to the right of previous lines

The **vertical-lr** option was not supported under the SVG 1.1 writing modes. It is used in a few Asian languages, and will also make layout of vertical labels in diagrams and data visualizations much more natural for people accustomed to left-to-right reading.

The orientation of characters within vertical text will be controlled by a new **text-orientation** property, which has the following options:

`mixed`
Use vertical glyphs when available, otherwise rotate 90° clockwise; equivalent to **glyph-orientation-vertical: auto**.

`upright`
Use vertical glyphs when available, otherwise use the horizontal glyphs set upright one below another; equivalent to **glyph-orientation-vertical: 0**.

`sideways-right`
Use horizontal text layout, rotated 90° clockwise; for left-to-right text, this is equivalent to **glyph-orientation-vertical: 90**; for right-to-left text, the text would now go from bottom to top.

`sideways-left`
Use horizontal text layout, rotated 90° counterclockwise; this is *not* equivalent to **glyph-orientation-vertical: 270**; for left-to-right text, the text would now go from bottom to top.

`sideways`
Use **sideways-left** or **sideways-right** according to the **writing-mode** (*not* **direction**), so that the top and bottom of each line of characters matches the top and bottom of the paragraph; this is what you would normally want for setting vertical labels in normally horizontal scripts.

`use-glyph-orientation`

> Use the SVG `glyph-orientation-vertical` and `glyph-orientation-horizontal` properties if they are supported.

The `use-glyph-orientation` value would be the default for SVG text, but is not expected to be implemented in browsers that do not already support the glyph orientation properties; other browsers would treat it equivalent to **mixed**, which is the default for non-SVG content.

If you have content that uses the SVG 1.1 vertical writing properties, you can maximize support in a future-proof manner, by adding the CSS 3 style properties to your code. If you are already using CSS style rules to apply the SVG properties, just add the CSS 3 values immediately after; browsers that do not recognize the new syntax will fall back to the previous declaration. When the SVG code uses presentation attributes, as in Example 7-2, you can apply the corresponding CSS rules using attribute selectors:

```
[writing-mode="tb"]{
    writing-mode: vertical-rl;
}
[glyph-orientation-vertical="0"]{
    text-orientation: upright;
}
```

Again, these values will be ignored if CSS 3 writing modes are not supported; if the new syntax *is* recognized, the CSS style rules will replace the values set in presentation attributes.

Until vertical writing modes are well supported, SVG does have one well-supported option for setting sideways text: rotate the entire text element using `transform`. To set text upright, top to bottom, the most reliable approach is to give x and dy values for each character. To create mixed orientation text, you can rotate the text element as a whole with transformations, then back-rotate individual characters with the `rotate` attribute, and finally, correct the spacing with dx.

Using this approach, we can create Figure 7-3, which looks almost the same as Figure 7-2, but works in all the major web browsers; the screenshot is from Firefox 40. The rather ugly markup required to create the layout is given in Example 7-3.

Figure 7-3. Vertical SVG text using transformations and character-by-character positions

Example 7-3. Simulating vertical writing mode using well-supported SVG features

```
<svg xmlns="http://www.w3.org/2000/svg"
    xmlns:xlink="http://www.w3.org/1999/xlink"
    width="4.3in" height="4.5in">
    <title>Faking Vertical Writing Modes</title>
    <style type="text/css">
        svg {
            font: 20px sans-serif;
            stroke-width: 2px;
        }
        text {
```

```
            fill: currentColor;
        }
    </style>
    <defs>
        <circle id="anchor" r="3px" fill="currentColor"
                stroke="currentColor" fill-opacity="0.5"/>
    </defs>
    <rect fill="#CEE" width="100%" height="100%" />
    <g color="darkGreen" text-anchor="start">
        <g id="sample" fill="currentColor" >
            <use xlink:href="#anchor" x="1em" y="2em" />
            <text x="1em" y="2em" >Hi, SVG World!</text>          ❶

            <use xlink:href="#anchor" x="2.5em" y="3em" />
            <text x="2.5em" y="3em" >您好 SVG 世界！</text>
        </g>
        <g id="rotated" transform="translate(0,50)" >
            <use xlink:href="#anchor" x="1em" y="2em" />
            <text x="2em" y="-1em" transform="rotate(90)"
                    dy="1ex"
                    >Hi, SVG World!</text>                        ❷

            <use xlink:href="#anchor" x="2.5em" y="3em" />
            <text x="3em" y="-2.5em" transform="rotate(90)"
                    rotate="-90 -90 0 0 0 -90 -90 -90"
                    dx="1em 0 -0.7em 0 0 1em" dy="1ex"
                    >您好 SVG 世界！</text>                        ❸
        </g>
        <g id="upright" transform="translate(100,50)" >
            <use xlink:href="#anchor" x="1em" y="2em" />
            <text  x="1em 1em 1em 1em 1em 1em 1em
                      1em 1em 1em 1em 1em 1em 1em"
                    dy="1em 1em 1em 1em 1em 1em 1em
                      1em 1em 1em 1em 1em 1em 1em"
                    text-anchor="middle"
                    y="2em" >Hi, SVG World!</text>                 ❹

            <use xlink:href="#anchor" x="2.5em" y="3em" />
            <text  x="2.5em 2.5em 2.5em 2.5em 2.5em 2.5em 2.5em
                      2.5em"
                    dy="1em 1em 1em 1em 1em 1em 1em 1em"
                    text-anchor="middle"
                    y="3em" >您好 SVG 世界！</text>                ❺
        </g>
    </g>
    <g color="darkRed" text-anchor="end"
      transform="translate(200,0)" >
        <use xlink:href="#sample" transform="translate(140,0)" />
        <use xlink:href="#rotated" transform="translate(0,300)" /> ❻

        <g id="upright-end" transform="translate(100,350)"
```

```
                text-anchor="middle">
            <use xlink:href="#anchor" x="1em" y="2em" />
            <text  x="1em 1em 1em 1em 1em 1em 1em
                      1em 1em 1em 1em 1em 1em 1em"
                   dy="-13em 1em 1em 1em 1em 1em 1em
                         1em 1em 1em 1em 1em 1em 1em"
                   y="2em" >Hi, SVG World!</text>

            <use xlink:href="#anchor" x="2.5em" y="3em" />
            <text  x="2.5em 2.5em 2.5em 2.5em 2.5em 2.5em 2.5em
                      2.5em"
                   dy="-7em 1em 1em 1em 1em 1em 1em 1em"
                   y="3em" >您好 SVG 世界！</text>
        </g>
    </g>

</svg>
```

❼

❶ The horizontal text samples are the same as in Example 7-2.

❷ The sideways Latin text is created with a rotational transforma-
    tion. However, because the rotation also affects the x and y
    attributes on the <text> element, they have to be changed as
    well: the anchor point is (1em,2em) in the base coordinate sys-
    tem, but (2em,−1em) in the rotated coordinate system. Finally, a
    dy attribute shifts the text to be approximately centered under
    the anchor (a vertical shift in the rotated coordinate system cre-
    ates a horizontal shift on the page) to match the default behav-
    ior of top-to-bottom text.

❸ The mixed-orientation Chinese and English text is more com-
    plicated. Again, the text as a whole is rotated, and the x and y
    attributes adjusted accordingly. The rotate attribute turns the
    Chinese characters upright again, and then the dx value corrects
    the spacing when switching between rotated and un-rotated
    characters; in the rotated coordinate system, dx adjustments
    move letters up and down on the page. The dy attribute again
    shifts the entire string to center it under the anchor point.

❹ The upright vertical text is created entirely with character-by-
    character positioning, each letter reset to the absolute x-
    coordinate and offset to a new line with the dy value. The letters
    are centered under the original anchor point with text-

anchor="middle". Because this is still technically horizontal text, the text-anchor property controls horizontal alignment.

❺ For fully upright text, no special strategy is required for mixed Latin and Chinese characters. The only difference compared to the all-Latin text is that the x and y positions use a different anchor point, and there are fewer characters overall.

❻ The rotated text can be reused and switched to end alignment simply by changing the inherited value of text-anchor. The transformations on the <use> element and the reused <g> add together, so the translation on the <use> has been reduced accordingly.

❼ Switching to end alignment requires more work for the upright text. Changing text-anchor does not have the intended effect; these are single-character horizontal text chunks for anchoring purposes. Instead, the initial dy value is adjusted as required to shift the entire text string to the correct side of the anchor point.

Although the final appearance is acceptable, the code is repetitive and difficult to maintain. Any change to the text content or layout will require many coordinated changes in positioning attributes.

The code also includes adjustments for one feature we have not discussed yet. In horizontal text, the anchor point is by default aligned with the bottom of the Latin letters. In contrast, vertical text is by default centered around the anchor point (this is changed for sideways text in CSS Writing Modes). Both of these are examples of *alignment baselines*, which are the topic of Chapter 8.

Lining Up

Text layout, as we have seen, involves both vertical and horizontal positioning. It only stands to reason that there should be control over both vertical and horizontal alignment.

The text-anchor property controls how a string of characters (text chunk) is aligned around the anchor point, *in the direction of text flow* (the "inline progression direction" in the specifications). In other words, it sets horizontal alignment for horizontal text and vertical alignment for vertical text. However, you often also want to control how the text is aligned in the perpendicular direction—for horizontal text, you want to control the vertical alignment.

This is especially true in graphical layouts. In flow diagrams or system architecture diagrams, one of the more complex tasks in putting things together is accurately centering lines of text. Not only do you have to center the content horizontally, but also vertically. Setting a y="50%" value is not sufficient, as it makes the text appear top-heavy: in most scripts, the part above the baseline is much larger than the part below.

It isn't only a problem in technical drawings. The quintessential interface device, the button, usually consists of text within a shape. Centering text within such buttons can be difficult at the best of times.

Again, the matter of alignment is complicated by the many different writing systems in use around the world—and around the World Wide Web. Latin letters (such as the ones you're now reading) normally sit upon their baseline, with the occasional tail hanging down; very few letters extend the full height defined by the font-size. In contrast, most Chinese traditional characters fit in equal-sized boxes, and are aligned either along the base of that box or its center line. A few scripts are aligned along the top—or a line close to the top—with the majority of each character hanging down.

Baseline Basics

Baselines are important in SVG for two reasons. First and most importantly, the baseline is used to align the text with the anchor point. Second, baselines are used to align differently styled sections of a text string together. When you change scripts, fonts, or font sizes, the different baselines of the characters will be spaced differently; they cannot *all* line up with the equivalent positions on the characters in the rest of the text.

SVG relies on two style properties to control baseline alignment: dominant-baseline to set the main baseline used for aligning a text element on a page, and alignment-baseline to set the baseline for aligning nested text with the parent text element. Both properties have equivalents in the XSLFO formatting language for printed documents; they are now being integrated into general CSS layout through the CSS Inline Layout Module. Neither property is inherited by default, although they *should* affect nested content indirectly.

At the time of writing, Internet Explorer has not implemented any of the baseline alignment properties; all text uses the default `alphabetic` baseline. The other browsers' implementations are incomplete and inconsistent:

- Firefox does not recognize `alignment-baseline` at all; however, when `dominant-baseline` is set on a nested `<tspan>`, it is treated the way `alignment-baseline` should be: that baseline in the nested text is aligned with the equivalent point on the parent text.

- WebKit/Blink browsers treat `alignment-baseline` as a synonym for `dominant-baseline`; when either value is set on a nested `<tspan>`, that baseline in the nested text is aligned with the current y-position of the text (or x-position for vertical text).

With those warnings in mind, you probably *do not* want to use the baseline properties for centering a single span of consistently styled text in a button. In an ideal world, that would be a perfect use case for a central baseline, but right now it is not reliable. Instead, use the dy property with a value of between 0.5ex and 0.5em, depending on whether you're using mostly lowercase letters, uppercase letters, or ideographic characters. This will shift the text down until it is approximately centered around your anchor point.

Where the baseline alignment properties are essential, however, is when you're mixing text of different sizes. In that situation, improving the alignment for most users may be worth losing perfect alignment in Internet Explorer.

To ensure a consistent result in the other browsers, follow these guidelines until implementations improve:

- Use `dominant-baseline`, *not* `alignment-baseline`
- Set all `<tspan>` elements to `dominant-baseline: inherit`

The `inherit` value is essential for Blink/WebKit; without it, any `<tspan>` content will be reset to use the default baseline relative to the text-anchor point.

So what are your baseline options? There are eight possibilities in the SVG specifications:

`alphabetic`
Align along the bottom of most letters in Western scripts

`ideographic`
Align along the bottom of East Asian ideographic characters; for Western scripts, this usually means the bottom of the *descenders* (the tails that drop down below the alphabetic baseline in letters such as "g" and "y")

`middle`
Align down the middle of lowercase letters in Western scripts, one-half the ex-height above the alphabetic baseline

`central`
Align halfway between the top and bottom of East Asian ideographic characters; in Western scripts, this is approximately halfway between the top of *ascenders* (the projections above the ex-height in lowercase letters such as "f") and the bottom of descenders

`hanging`
Align along a baseline in the upper half of characters; the hanging baseline is used in some Indic scripts where most letters have a strong horizontal line at this point

`mathematical`
Align along a baseline that looks best for setting mathematical equations with fractions and other characters; when the dominant baseline is alphabetic, this will usually be halfway between the alphabetic baseline and the ascender height; it should match up with the lines in mathematical symbols such as +, −, and ÷

`text-before-edge`
Align along the top edge of all normal (unaccented) characters, or the right edge for vertical text

`text-after-edge`

Align along the bottom edge (or left edge for vertical text) of all normal characters; this is usually the same as `ideographic`

The exact positions of each baseline should ideally be defined in the font file. If they aren't, the browser should make a best guess based on the properties that are specified in the font.

Firefox currently treats `mathematical` as a synonym for `central` and `hanging` as a synonym for `text-before-edge`, if the font does not specify these baselines explicity. Versions prior to 40 also treated `middle` equivalent to `central`.

In well-designed fonts, the baselines are given as a matrix of values. If the overall layout (`dominant-baseline`) uses the ideographic baseline, the position of central and mathematical baselines (for `alignment-baseline`) may be different than if the overall layout uses an alphabetic baseline. Similarly, when switching between different fonts, the font from the parent element should be used to determine the dominant baseline position, and then the baseline from the nested font should be aligned with it.

Versions of Blink browsers prior to Chromium 44 do not correctly handle baselines other than `alphabetic` when the browser window is zoomed to any value other than 100%. As mentioned in Chapter 7, the same problem shows up with vertical text.

Example 8-1 demonstrates all the different baselines for text with a mixture of fonts, sizes, and scripts. It draws gray lines in the background to mark the position of the anchor point and therefore of the baseline. Figure 8-1 shows the SVG as it appears in Chrome (version 44), including the subtle differences between `middle`, `central`, and `mathematical`.

Example 8-1. Using alignment baselines to lay out SVG text

```
<svg xmlns="http://www.w3.org/2000/svg"
     xmlns:xlink="http://www.w3.org/1999/xlink"
     width="415" height="250" viewBox="0 0 415 250">
```

'alphabetic' alignment您好   'ideographic' alignment您好

'middle' alignment您好   'central' alignment您好

'hanging' alignment您好   'mathematical' alignment您好

                                  'text-after-edge' alignment您好
'text-before-edge' alignment您好

Figure 8-1. SVG text with various baselines

```
<title>Text Baseline Comparison</title>
<style>
    svg {
        text-anchor: middle;
        font-family: Arial, Helvetica, sans-serif;
        font-size: 12pt;
    }
    line {
        stroke: lightGray;
        stroke-width: 2px;
    }
    .small {
        font-size: 75%;
        font-family: Times New Roman, Times, serif;
    }
    tspan {
        dominant-baseline: inherit;
    }
</style>
<defs>
    <line id="baseline" x1="-100" x2="100"/>
    <line id="spine" y2="250" />
</defs>
<g transform="translate(105,0)">
    <use xlink:href="#spine"/>
    <g transform="translate(0,50)">
        <use xlink:href="#baseline"/>
        <text dominant-baseline="alphabetic">'alphabetic'
            <tspan class="small">alignment 您好</tspan></text>
```

```
    </g>
    <g transform="translate(0,100)">
        <use xlink:href="#baseline"/>
        <text dominant-baseline="middle">'middle'
            <tspan class="small">alignment 您好</tspan></text>
    </g>
    <g transform="translate(0,150)">
        <use xlink:href="#baseline"/>
        <text dominant-baseline="hanging">'hanging'
            <tspan class="small">alignment 您好</tspan></text>
    </g>
    <g transform="translate(0,200)">
        <use xlink:href="#baseline"/>
        <text dominant-baseline="text-before-edge"
            >'text-before-edge'
            <tspan class="small">alignment 您好</tspan></text>
    </g>
</g>
<g transform="translate(310,0)">
    <use xlink:href="#spine"/>
    <g transform="translate(0,50)">
        <use xlink:href="#baseline"/>
        <text dominant-baseline="ideographic">'ideographic'
            <tspan class="small">alignment 您好</tspan></text>
    </g>
    <g transform="translate(0,100)">
        <use xlink:href="#baseline"/>
        <text dominant-baseline="central">'central'
            <tspan class="small">alignment 您好</tspan></text>
    </g>
    <g transform="translate(0,150)">
        <use xlink:href="#baseline"/>
        <text dominant-baseline="mathematical">'mathematical'
            <tspan class="small">alignment 您好</tspan></text>
    </g>
    <g transform="translate(0,200)">
        <use xlink:href="#baseline"/>
        <text dominant-baseline="text-after-edge"
            >'text-after-edge'
            <tspan class="small">alignment 您好</tspan></text>
    </g>
    </g>
    </g>
</svg>
```

The default `dominant-baseline` is `alphabetic`, which is what we have seen in all examples prior to Example 8-1.

The default for `alignment-baseline` was supposed to be to use the intrinsic baseline defined in the font file for each particular character; given the overall poor support for `alignment-baseline`, it's not suprising that this doesn't happen. Firefox's default behavior is similar to the expected behavior of `alignment-baseline: baseline`, which is to use the parent's dominant baseline to align the nested text. The `dominant-baseline: inherit` rule creates the same behavior in WebKit/Blink.

Baselines apply to vertical text as well. The default baseline for vertical text is `central`: WebKit and Blink browsers follow this, and center vertical text under (or over) the anchor point (as was shown in Figure 7-2, the vertical text example in Chapter 7).

Internet Explorer (with no baseline support) always uses a rotated alphabetic baseline for vertical text, which means it lays out characters to the left of the anchor.

In a well-designed font that includes characters frequently used in vertical text, explicit baselines will be defined for vertical text alignment. However, the browser or other layout program *should* calculate approximations if the font data is not provided.

Super (and Sub) Baselines

Of course, sometimes you don't want the baseline in smaller text to perfectly line up with the same point in larger text. For instance, you may want it to appear as a subscript or superscript. SVG uses the `baseline-shift` property to handle this situation.

The `baseline-shift` value can be specified as an absolute length, a percentage of the parent element's `line-height` (which for SVG 1.1 is always the `font-size`), or as one of the keywords `sub` or `super`. The property is inherited, and can be specified as a presentation attribute or CSS rule.

The `baseline-shift` property is not currently supported in either Firefox or Internet Explorer.

Although you can always shift an SVG `<tspan>` using the dy property, it is often difficult to shift *back* to the original baseline after the span is over, particularly when the spans have different font sizes. In contrast, a `baseline-shift` effect does not change the current text position for the rest of the text.

 For `baseline-shift` on horizontal text, positive values shift the text *up* and negative values shift it down. For dy, the reverse is true, as the *y*-axis increases going down.

Example 8-2 uses `baseline-shift` to position subscripts in a chemical formula as well as superscripts used to identify footnotes. It uses a `mathematical` baseline for the formula, which results in more pleasing subscripts; as shown in Figure 8-2, they are centered around the alphabetical baseline of the letters.

Example 8-2. Using baseline-shift to create subscript and superscript text

```
<?xml version="1.0" encoding="UTF-8"?>
<svg xmlns="http://www.w3.org/2000/svg"
     width="410px" height="100px" viewBox="0 0 410 100">
    <title>Baseline Shift in SVG Text</title>
    <style type="text/css">
    tspan {
        dominant-baseline: inherit;                          ❶
    }
    .formula {
        font-size: 22pt;
        text-anchor: middle;
        dominant-baseline: mathematical;
    }
    .super {
        font-size: 50%;
        baseline-shift: super;
    }
    .sub {
        font-size: 50%;
        baseline-shift: sub;
    }
    .footnote {
        dominant-baseline: alphabetic;
        font-size: 14pt;
    }
    .footnote-divider {
        stroke: dimGray;
        stroke-width: 2px;
    }
```

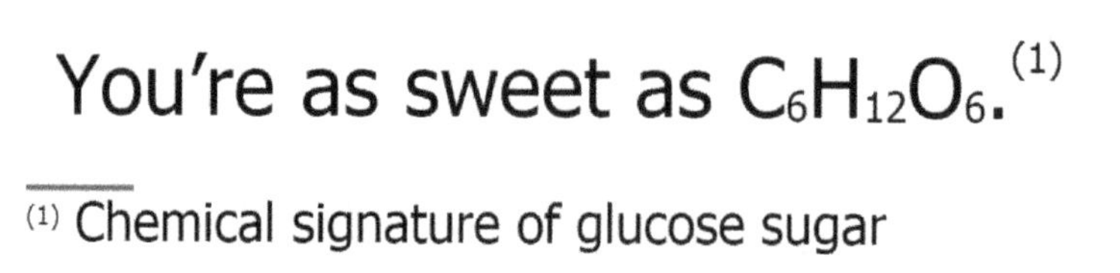

You're as sweet as $C_6H_{12}O_6$.[1]

[1] Chemical signature of glucose sugar

Figure 8-2. SVG text with subscripts and superscripts

```
    </style>
    <rect fill="lightYellow" width="100%" height="100%" />
    <text x="50%" y="1em" class="formula">You&#8217;re as sweet  ❷
        as C<tspan class="sub">6</tspan>H<tspan
        class="sub">12</tspan>O<tspan class="sub">6</tspan
        >.<tspan class="super">(1)</tspan></text>          ❸
    <g transform="translate(10,70)">
        <line x2="40" class="footnote-divider" />
        <text dy="1em" class="footnote"><tspan
            class="super">(1)</tspan>
            Chemical signature of glucose sugar</text>
    </g>
</svg>
```

❶ Because we're changing the `dominant-baseline` on text elements, we need to be sure that the nested `<tspan>` elements will follow suit in WebKit/Blink browsers (which are the only ones that currently support `baseline-shift`).

❷ The `&#8217;` entity references the Unicode character for a curly apostrophe (right single quote). Because this is an SVG file, you cannot use the HTML `&rsquo;` entity.

❸ To avoid introducing whitespace in the actual text content, the code is broken into lines *inside* the markup tags.

There are a couple of subtleties at play here. The first point worth considering is that, unlike the HTML `<sub>` and `<super>` elements, SVG will not automatically set `font-size` to a smaller size for text with super/sub baselines. As is typically the case, SVG gives you greater granular control over the visual appearance than HTML, but at the cost of requiring that you define each style change yourself.

Because the `sub` and `super` classes use percentages to scale down the `font-size`, nested elements can compound the effect. For instance, if one mathematical power was raised to another mathematical power, the next superscript up would be half again as small as the first, or $\frac{1}{4}$ of the original font size.

Baseline Alignment Control

The SVG baseline alignment properties were quickly recognized as a model that CSS text layout should emulate; however, progress on a standard has been halting. A 2002 draft CSS module incorporated them, but never progressed. It was eventually replaced in 2014 by the CSS Inline Layout Module Level 3, which is approaching the final draft stage at the time of writing.

The CSS module adopts the **dominant-baseline**, **alignment-baseline**, and **baseline-shift** properties with minor changes:

- The values **text-before-edge** and **text-after-edge** would be replaced by **text-top** and **text-bottom** to correspond with the equivalent values for the **vertical-align** property. They would still apply to vertical text in a before/after manner.

- The default for **alignment-baseline** would be **baseline**; the hypothetical SVG default **auto** behavior is not currently included as an option.

- Three additional values for **alignment-baseline** are introduced, again based on the **vertical-align** property (which controls the alignment of inline boxes): **top**, **center**, and **bottom**. These would be useful if there were a series of nested elements with various baseline offsets or superscripts/subscripts (such as in mathematical equations); the overall top, bottom, or center of the formatted text would be aligned with the same part of the main text line.

- The following (currently unsupported) keywords for the **dominant-baseline** property are dropped: **use-script**, **no-change**, and **reset-size**.

The CSS module would nonetheless *discourage* the use of **alignment-baseline** and **baseline-shift** in favor of **vertical-align**, which would be redefined as a shorthand combining those two properties.

The **vertical-align** property—as currently defined in CSS 2.1 for inline text layout—already supports superscripts, subscripts, and other fixed offsets, as well as `baseline` (default, usually alphabetical baseline), `middle`, `text-top` and `text-bottom`, and `top` or `bottom`. It would be expanded to include all the specific baseline options.

Mimicking Baseline Control

Given the poor support for baseline control in web browsers, how can you create SVGs for the Web with subscripts, superscripts, and other combinations of text of different sizes? Once again, you can replace the missing layout properties using SVG's manual text positioning attributes. Once again, the resulting markup is not pretty.

The dy attribute shifts the baseline of (horizontal) text relative to the anchor point. As mentioned earlier in the chapter, this can be used to approximately center text around the anchor point. However, a dy offset affects all subsequent characters in the text. If you switch font sizes and want to re-center the alignment, you'll need to first cancel out the adjustment from the previous font size. If you want a temporary baseline shift for a subscript or superscript, you'll need to cancel it out at the end.

In order to correctly cancel out a text positioning attribute that uses font-relative units (em or ex), you'll need to apply the reverse dy value to the same element or an element with the same font. Because dy values only have an effect when applied to a character, you may need to use the non-breaking space ( ), zero-width space (), or zero-width non-joiner (‌) characters to provide a non-collapsible whitespace character or a character that does not affect layout at all.

When SVG is inline in HTML, you can use the defined entities   for the non-breaking space and ‌ for the zero-width non-joiner character. The numerical versions are required in pure SVG documents.

Example 8-3 uses these techniques to create a cross-browser version of Example 8-2. The code makes extensive use of the zero-width non-joiner as a reset character. For the subscript numbers, the reset is contained within the same <tspan> and multiple values are given

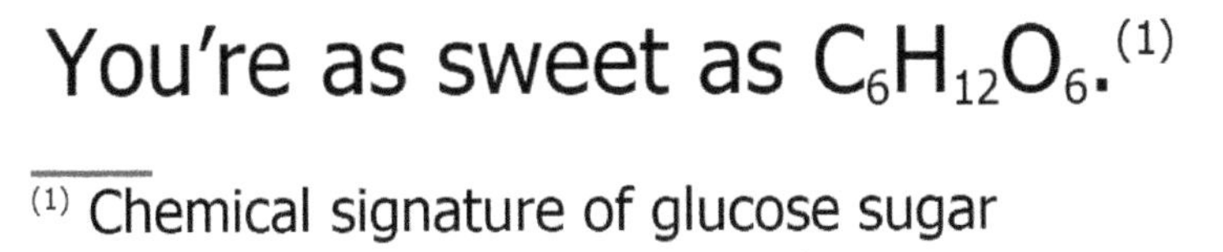

You're as sweet as $C_6H_{12}O_6$. [1]

[1] Chemical signature of glucose sugar

Figure 8-3. SVG text with manually created superscripts and subscripts

for dy. For the footnote superscript, an extra <tspan> is inserted (nested within the one that changes the font size) so that the dy attribute does not need to be padded with zeros for each superscript character. Figure 8-3 shows the end result.

Example 8-3. Using dy and zero-width characters to simulate baseline properties

```
<?xml version="1.0" encoding="UTF-8"?>
<svg xmlns="http://www.w3.org/2000/svg"
     width="410px" height="100px" viewBox="0 0 410 100">
    <title>Faking Baseline Shift in SVG Text</title>
    <style type="text/css">
    .formula {
        font-size: 22pt;
        text-anchor: middle;
    }
    .super, .sub {
        font-size: 50%;                              ❶
    }
    .footnote {
        font-size: 14pt;
    }
    .footnote-divider {
        stroke: dimGray;
        stroke-width: 2px;
    }
    </style>
    <rect fill="lightYellow" width="100%" height="100%" />
    <text x="50%" y="1em" dy="1ex" class="formula">You&#8217;re  ❷
        as sweet as C<tspan class="sub" dy="0.5ex -0.5ex"
        >6&#8204;</tspan>H<tspan class="sub" dy="0.5ex 0 -0.5ex"
        >12&#8204;</tspan>O<tspan class="sub" dy="0.5ex -0.5ex"
        >6&#8204;</tspan>.<tspan class="super" dy="-0.8em"
        >(1)</tspan></text>                          ❸
    <g transform="translate(10,70)">
```

```
            <line x2="40" class="footnote-divider" />
            <text y="1em" class="footnote">                                    ❹
                <tspan class="super" dy="-0.8em">(1)<tspan dy="0.8em"
                >&#8204;</tspan></tspan>
                Chemical signature of glucose sugar</text>
        </g>
</svg>
```

❶ The styles have been simplified to remove the poorly supported baseline properties.

❷ The mathematical baseline for the text as a whole is approximated with a single dy value.

❸ The subscripts now have dy attributes and extra zero-width characters at the end of the text content. For the single-digit subscripts, the dy value consists of one downward (positive) shift followed by an equal and opposite shift for the zero-width character. The multidigit subscript "12" requires an extra dy value to maintain the shift for the second character. Finally, the superscript at the end of the line is shifted up with a negative dy value; because no characters follow it, the baseline is not reset.

❹ In contrast, for the superscript in the footnote, a reset *is* required. An extra <tspan> is inserted with a single zero-width character to make the shift.

Again, the workaround creates an acceptable appearance, but requires confusing and difficult-to-maintain markup.

CHAPTER 9

Beyond Straight Lines

Baselines ensure that glyphs are positioned to create a pleasing line of text. However, we've already said that, in graphical layout, you don't always *want* text to display in perfectly straight lines. Sometimes it's fun to make text move out of those boring lines and into more complex curves—circles, spirals, around the edges of various objects, and so forth.

This chapter introduces the `<textPath>` element, which allows you to use SVG path geometry to describe complex text layouts.

Creating Curved Text

We've shown (in Chapter 5) how you can position and rotate individual characters. For some simple designs, that's enough. Example 9-1 spaces the letters of the word "Sunrise" in a semicircle, each letter positioned every 30° and rotated to match, as shown in Figure 9-1.

Example 9-1. Arranging letters around a shape with character position attributes

```
<svg xmlns="http://www.w3.org/2000/svg"
     xmlns:xlink="http://www.w3.org/1999/xlink"
     xml:lang="en"
     width="4in" height="2.3in" viewBox="0 0 400 230">
    <title>Text Positioned in a Curve</title>
    <style type="text/css">
        text {
            font: bold italic 48px "Times New Roman", Times, serif;
```

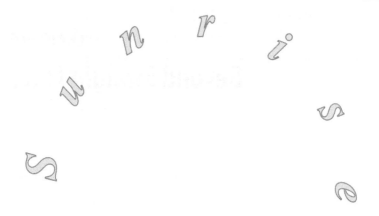

Figure 9-1. Curved text positioned with x, y, and rotate

```
          fill: gold;
          stroke: orangeRed;
      }
  </style>
  <rect fill="#CEE" width="100%" height="100%" />
  <g transform="translate(200,180)">                ❶
      <text x="-150 -130 -75 0 75 130 150"
            y="0 -75 -130 -150 -130 -75 0"
            rotate="-90 -60 -30 0 30 60 90"
            >Sunrise</text>                         ❷
  </g>
</svg>
```

❶ To make the trigonometry *slightly* easier, the coordinate system origin is translated to the center of the semicircle.

❷ There are seven letters in "Sunrise," so there are seven values in each of the positioning attribute lists.

The exact positions of each letter required a little bit of trigonometry to calculate. Even then, it doesn't look quite right: because the letters *start* at the specified anchor point, the final "e" sticks out below the starting "S" even though their anchors are on the same horizontal line. Using `text-anchor: middle` doesn't help; it centers each letter over the anchor point *before* rotating them, so they end up shifted to the side, not shifted around the circle.

If we had more letters, we'd need more trigonometry, and longer lists of x, y, and `rotate` attributes. And if we had enough letters that we wanted the word to look like a continuous string of text, we'd have to deal with the fact that each letter should be spaced differently according to its own unique dimensions. This clearly isn't a practical solution for pleasing text layout.

For cursive scripts such as Arabic, there's another problem with absolutely positioning letters: no matter how close each letter is to the next, they are rendered as isolated letters, not parts of a continuous word.

This is where text on a path comes in handy. Text on a path is exactly what it says—each letter is placed such that its baseline is on the tangent of a curve, spaced out along that curve according to the normal spacing of that text sequence.

 Although text on a path *should* be perfect for creating decorative layouts with cursive text, actual browser implementations are another matter, particularly for right-to-left scripts such as Arabic.

SVG text on a path is created with the `<textPath>` element. The content of the `<textPath>` is aligned along the outline of a separate `<path>` element. Which path to use is specified with an `xlink:href` attribute.

 Just like a `<tspan>`, a `<textPath>` *must* be within a `<text>` element; it does not draw anything on its own.

Example 9-2 arranges the longer string "from Sunrise to Sunset" around a semicircular path (actually a cubic Bézier curve). The result is shown in Figure 9-2.

Figure 9-2. Curved text positioned along a path

Example 9-2. Arranging a text string around a shape with textPath

```
<svg xmlns="http://www.w3.org/2000/svg"
     xmlns:xlink="http://www.w3.org/1999/xlink"
     xml:lang="en"
     width="4in" height="2.3in" viewBox="0 0 400 230">
  <title>Text on a Curved Path</title>
  <style type="text/css">
      text {
          font: bold italic 48px "Times New Roman", Times, serif;
          fill: gold;
          stroke: orangeRed;
      }
  </style>
  <rect fill="#CEE" width="100%" height="100%" />
  <path id="path" d="M50,200 C50,0 350,0 350,200"
        fill="none" stroke="darkOrange" />
  <text>
      <textPath xlink:href="#path">from Sunrise
          to Sunset</textPath>
  </text>
</svg>
```

The letters in Figure 9-2 are spaced much more smoothly than you could expect to achieve by placing each character yourself.

Blink/WebKit browsers currently render each letter within text on a path as if it was its own text chunk. This doesn't affect the spacing, but it has other consequences. For right-to-left scripts within a left-to-right layout, this means that the letters are not rearranged into the correct reading order. In cursive scripts, it also means that the isolated glyph forms for each letter are used instead of the word forms.

The path itself is stroked in Example 9-2, but it does not have to be; you can define the path within a `<defs>` section without drawing it at all. Here, we draw it to emphasize that the baseline of the text is aligned with the path. If you used a different baseline, the characters would move in or out relative to the curve.

Regardless of whether the path itself was drawn to the screen or not, the text will be positioned as if the path was drawn in the same coordinate system as the `<text>` element itself.

Positioning on a Path

The text string in Example 9-2 doesn't quite fit the full length of the path, making it appear slightly off-balance. A `text-anchor: middle` setting could center the text, but only if we can correctly position the anchor point. By default, it's at the start of the path. If we centered the text around that point, half of it would disappear off the start of the path.

Any text that extends beyond the length of the path—at the beginning or end—will not be drawn at all.

The `startOffset` attribute of a `<textPath>` element defines the position along the path at which the text should be anchored. It can be given as a length—measured from the normal start of the path—or as a percentage of the path's length. To center text within the path length, you can therefore use `text-anchor: middle` with a `startOffset` of 50%, as follows:

```
<text text-anchor="middle">
    <textPath xlink:href="#path" startOffset="50%"
```

Figure 9-3. Curved text centered on a path

```
            >from Sunrise to Sunset</textPath>
    </text>
```

Figure 9-3 shows the much more balanced result of this change.

The `startOffset` attribute is particularly useful when arranging text around an existing shape, which might not have been drawn with the start of the text in mind. When animated, a changing `startOffset` can create a marquee effect, sliding text the length of the path.

 Blink/WebKit browsers currently treat negative `startOffset` values as 0, and do not draw any text with a `startOffset` greater than 100% of the path length, even when using an `end` value for `text-anchor`. This rather limits the potential for scrolling marquees of appearing and disappearing text.

On closed shapes (such as a complete circle), be aware that text will not continue from the end of the path back to the beginning. To position text across this seam in the path definition, create a version of the path with the entire path string duplicated. Then reduce any

Figure 9-4. Arabic text on a path, with drop-shadow filter

percentage values for startOffset by half, to account for the fact that the path is now twice as long.[1]

The SVG 1.1 specifications did not define how startOffset—or text paths in general—would work for right-to-left text direction. Firefox is currently the only browser that provides legible results with correct bidirectional ordering.

Internet Explorer and Blink/WebKit browsers do not correctly process right-to-left and bidirectional text on a path. For cursive scripts (such as Arabic) Blink/WebKit also use the isolated glyph versions of each character.

Even for Firefox (version 40) the startOffset value is used as an *end*-offset position when text-anchor is start and the reverse for a text-anchor of end. This ensures that text is still visible with the default offset value of 0, but it is otherwise un-intuitive and inconsistent with the rest of SVG text layout.

Figure 9-4 shows how Arabic text on a path could look (screenshot from Firefox 40). The code is given in Example 9-3.

---

1 Thanks to Israel Eisenberg for the doubled-path solution for text on a closed shape.

Example 9-3. Displaying right-to-left cursive text within textPath

```
<svg xmlns="http://www.w3.org/2000/svg"
    xmlns:xlink="http://www.w3.org/1999/xlink"
    width="4in" height="2.3in" viewBox="0 0 400 230">
    <title xml:lang="en">Arabic Text on a Curved Path</title>
    <style type="text/css">
        text {
            font: bold italic 48px "Times New Roman", Times, serif;
            fill: gold;
            stroke: orangeRed;
        }
        @supports (filter: drop-shadow(0 0 0)){
            text {
                stroke: none;
                filter: drop-shadow(orangeRed 0.5px 1px 1px);
            }
        }
    </style>
    <rect fill="#CEE" width="100%" height="100%" />
    <path id="path" d="M50,200 C50,0 350,0 350,200"
        fill="none" stroke="darkOrange" />
    <text text-anchor="middle" dir="rtl" xml:lang="ar">
        <textPath xlink:href="#path" startOffset="50%"
            >جميل الخط النسخية على منحنى</textPath>
    </text>
</svg>
```

Although mostly similar to the centered version of Example 9-2, Example 9-3 uses a drop-shadow filter instead of a stroke to avoid interrupting the cursive connections. When letters are stroked, Firefox currently does not apply ligatures; even if it did, the strokes would include the edges between each glyph. A text shadow is not an improvement; it is also painted one glyph at a time, and so also overlaps the cursive connections. In contrast, the drop-shadow filter (introduced in the CSS Filters module, although it could also be created with SVG filter elements) is applied to the final shaped text, after combining all the glyphs into a single layer.

By comparison, Figure 9-5 shows the result with stroked text (also in Firefox 40). Although the connections between letters are much more awkward, this is still much closer to proper Arabic typography than any of the other web browsers are able to render at the time of writing.

The SVG 2 specifications will include new rules for how text on a path *should* behave. At the time of writing, they have not been final-

Figure 9-5. Arabic text on a path, with stroked letters

ized. One option would be to replace the default `startOffset` with an `auto` value that adapts according to the text direction.

Integrating Other Text Effects

Most of the other text features we have discussed so far can be used with text on a path, some with more success than others.

The text within a `<textPath>` element can have `<tspan>` sections that change the styling. Example 9-4 adds stroke and fill changes for the keywords in the string, as displayed in Figure 9-6.

Example 9-4. Styling text spans within textPath

```
<svg xmlns="http://www.w3.org/2000/svg"
    xmlns:xlink="http://www.w3.org/1999/xlink"
    xml:lang="en"
    width="4in" height="2.3in" viewBox="0 0 400 230">
    <title>Styled Text on a Curved Path</title>
    <style type="text/css">
        text {
            font: bold italic 48px "Times New Roman", Times, serif;
            fill: orangeRed;
        }
        .bright {
            fill: gold;
            stroke: orangeRed;
```

Figure 9-6. Curved text on a path, with styled spans

```
    }
</style>
<rect fill="#CEE" width="100%" height="100%" />
<path id="path" d="M50,200 C50,0 350,0 350,200"
      fill="none" stroke="darkOrange" />
<text text-anchor="middle">
    <textPath xlink:href="#path" startOffset="50%"
        >from
        <tspan class="bright">Sunrise</tspan>
        to
        <tspan class="bright">Sunset</tspan
            ></textPath>
</text>
</svg>
```

The styles on the <tspan> elements are applied with the `bright` class, to override the styles set on the <text> as a whole.

 Avoid setting styles using a CSS selector for the textPath tag name. Older Blink and WebKit browsers do not correctly match mixed-case tag names for SVG elements (case sensitive) that are inline in HTML 5 documents (case insensitive). The latest versions of both platforms have work-arounds for this problem.

If you can use <tspan> within <textPath>, can you use the normal text path positioning attributes? You can, but they don't have the normal effect. Instead of moving text horizontally or vertically, they move them along the path or perpendicular to the path.

 Although the x, y, dx, dy, and rotate positioning attributes on <text> and <tspan> *affect* the characters within a <textPath>, SVG 1.1 does not allow you to use these attributes directly on the <textPath> element.

For horizontal writing mode, therefore, a positive dx attribute moves characters futher along the path. A positive dy value shifts the text toward the inside of the path, while a negative dy value shifts it outward.

 Internet Explorer does not render any of the text if you use dx or dy in combination with text-anchor: middle; it renders these offsets correctly for text-anchor: start.

The other browsers have no problem with relative position attributes, but every browser tested was inconsistent and buggy when absolute positioning (x and y attributes) was used.

For vertical writing-mode, y-offsets move the text along the path and x-offsets move it perpendicularly. For right-to-left character sequences—whether or not they are embedded in a left-to-right layout—you would need to use negative dx values to add space between characters, the same as for normal SVG text.

 Browsers are currently very inconsistent about how <textPath> contents are laid out when the layout direction (i.e., direction property) is right to left. Unfortunately, the SVG 1.1 specifications did not discuss this situation carefully.

Example 9-5 uses dx and dy on both the <text> element that contains the <textPath> and the <tspan> elements within it. The resulting layout is shown in Figure 9-7.

Example 9-5. Using relative positioning attributes within textPath

```
<svg xmlns="http://www.w3.org/2000/svg"
     xmlns:xlink="http://www.w3.org/1999/xlink"
     width="4in" height="2.3in" viewBox="0 0 400 230">
    <title>Text Offset from a Curved Path</title>
    <style type="text/css">
        /* omitted to save space */                         ❶
    </style>
    <rect fill="#CEE" width="100%" height="100%" />
    <path id="path" d="M50,200 C50,0 350,0 350,200"
          fill="none" stroke="darkOrange" />
    <text dy="0.5ex" text-anchor="middle">                  ❷
        <textPath xlink:href="#path" startOffset="50%"
            >from
            <tspan class="bright" dy="-1ex" dx="10px"
            >Sunrise</tspan>                                 ❸
            <tspan dy="+1ex">to</tspan>                      ❹
            <tspan class="bright" dy="+1ex" dx="10px"
            >Sunset</tspan></textPath>                       ❺
    </text>
</svg>
```

❶ The styles would be the same as for Example 9-4.

❷ A dy attribute on the <text> element applies to the first character on the path. It shifts the first chunk of text on the path down
by 0.5ex, so the lowercase letters half-overlap the path. Using a
middle baseline would have had much the same effect, if it
could be relied upon for consistent browser support.

❸ The "Sunrise" span starts with some extra spacing (dx), and is
shifted outward (dy) by the full ex-height, so it ends up 0.5ex
beyond the path.

❹ A span around the word "to" is used to cancel out the dy value
and reset the baseline; if baseline-shift had better browser
support, it could have been used on "Sunrise" instead, and this
extra span would not be required.

❺ The "Sunset" span also starts with a dx offset, but its dy value
shifts it down, into the interior of the path.

In Figure 9-7, you'll notice that the letters in "Sunrise" are spaced
farther apart than usual, while the letters in "Sunset" look rather
cramped. This is because each letter is shifted perpendicular to its

Figure 9-7. Curved text on a path, with spans offset both along and perpendicular to the path

particular point on the path. On a curved path, those different perpendicular lines spread out on one side and come together on the other.

For tightly curved paths, the cramped or stretched effect can be visible even without a perpendicular shift. Convex curves, like this, will space out letters above the baseline and compress them below the baseline. Concave curves will do the opposite. As you can guess, the choice of baseline will also affect whether or not the letters end up uncomfortably spaced.

The SVG specifications include two other attributes to control text path layout, neither of which currently have an effect in browsers:

spacing
> How the glyphs should be positioned along the path. The default value supported in browsers is exact: each glyph takes up the same space on the path as it would in a straight line of text. The alternative value, auto, would allow the SVG rendering agent to adjust the spacing "in order to achieve visually appealing results," although what that means is not defined.

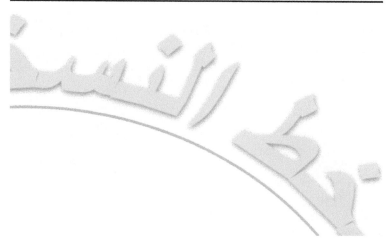

Figure 9-8. Discontinuities visible in cursive text on a path without stretch support

method

> How the text string should be bent to fit along the path. The default value supported in browsers is `align` (each glyph is aligned with the path without distorting it); the alternative, unsupported value is `stretch` (the tops and bottoms of each glyph are stretched or condensed to fill the available space).

The lack of support for the `stretch` method is particularly problematic with cursive scripts and fonts, whose glyphs may no longer overlap each other correctly when each character has a different rotation. In the Arabic text from Example 9-3, this is visible as cracks between adjacent glyphs, as shown in Figure 9-8 (a zoomed-in view of Figure 9-4). Nonetheless, the lack of support is perhaps not surprising, considering that there is no support anywhere else in SVG for a stretch-type distortion effect (technically called a non-affine transformation).

As mentioned briefly earlier, you can also use the x and y attributes to set absolute positioning within text on a path. These are only supposed to have an effect in the direction of the text, creating a new start offset; absolute positions perpendicular to the path would be ignored. In other words, for horizontal text on a path, the x attribute could be used to reposition the offset along the path. In combination

Figure 9-9. Multiline text arranged around a single path

with a dy attribute, this could (theoretically) be used to create multiline text above and below a path.

The specifications were short on details of how this would work, and browser implementations are correspondingly inconsistent. If you want to create multiline text on a path, use two <textPath> elements referencing the same <path> shape, with different dy offsets for each. Example 9-6 uses this approach to create the multiline text shown in Figure 9-9.

Example 9-6. Using multiple textPath elements to create multiline text on a path

```
<svg xmlns="http://www.w3.org/2000/svg"
     xmlns:xlink="http://www.w3.org/1999/xlink"
     xml:lang="en"
     width="4in" height="2.3in" viewBox="0 0 400 230">
    <title>Multiline Text on a Curved Path</title>
    <style type="text/css">
        text {
            font: bold italic 48px "Times New Roman", Times, serif;
            fill: gold;
            stroke: orangeRed;
        }
    </style>
    <rect fill="#CEE" width="100%" height="100%" />
    <path id="path" d="M50,200 C50,0 350,0 350,200"
          fill="none" stroke="darkOrange" />
```

```
<text text-anchor="middle">
    <textPath xlink:href="#path" startOffset="50%"
        letter-spacing="-2.5px"><tspan dy="-0.2em"
        >Text above a path</tspan></textPath>
    <textPath xlink:href="#path" startOffset="50%"
        letter-spacing="5px"><tspan dy="0.8em"
        >and below it, too!</tspan></textPath>
</text>
</svg>
```

The `<textPath>` elements in Example 9-6 use `letter-spacing` to adjust for the expansion and compression caused by the vertical offsets from the curved path. As mentioned previously, `letter-spacing` is not currently supported for SVG text in Firefox; the screenshot is from Chrome version 44.

Future Focus
Changes to Text on a Path

It's likely that SVG 2 will include a number of improvements and clarifications related to `<textPath>`, as well as a few new features.

Some changes that have already been decided:

- `<textPath>` will include a **d** attribute. It would allow you to specify the path directly, instead of having to define a separate `<path>` element.

- Alternatively, a `<textPath>` element could reference any shape element (circle, rectangle, polygon, etc.) instead of a `<path>`. Each shape has a canonical path representation that defines where a 0% start offset would be positioned.

- For closed shapes, text would continue smoothly from the end to the beginning.

- A new **side** attribute will allow you to define which side of the path the text should appear on, effectively reversing the path definition.

It will probably also be possible to specify positioning attributes directly on the `<textPath>` element, eliminating the need to have extra `<tspan>` elements.

The new specifications should also provide clearer definitions for details of text on a path layout that are currently inconsistently implemented (or not implemented at all), particularly with respect to right-to-left text layout.

CHAPTER 10

Fonts, Families, Faces

This book has so far covered, in extensive detail, all the ways in which you can control how letters (and other glyphs) are arranged within your SVG. The letters themselves, however, have been somewhat overlooked. This chapter addresses that gap. Letterforms are at least as important as layout in creating the final appearance of graphical text.

A full discussion of typography, fonts, and type selection in web design is a book unto itself. So we're not going to discuss how you would choose (or design!) a typeface for your graphic. Instead, this chapter focuses on how you can get the browser to use the font you prefer. Chapter 11 will then explain what you can do to minimize the impact if it uses a different font regardless of your style settings.

Generic Styles

The primary way to select a font, and therefore control the character style, is with the `font-family` style property. It is an inherited style that may be specified as an SVG presentation attribute or CSS style rule. With CSS rules, `font-family` may be set directly or as part of the `font` shorthand. However it is set, the value is a comma-separated list of font-family names, ending with a generic fallback font description.

Most of the examples in this book have simply used the generic names to describe what type of font should be used. These keywords are defined in core CSS, and describe some of the most basic distinctions between font types. Browsers are expected to provide fonts for the five core generic font types defined in CSS:

serif

שלום העולם! 你 Hello, World!
好
مرحبا أيها العالم! ! Привет мир!

A font with formal flourishes on the strokes of the glyphs, usually with variation in the thickness of the stroke. For Latin scripts (like the letters you are reading), the font will have *serifs*, small horizontal lines at the top and bottom of strokes.

sans-serif

שלום העולם! 你 Hello, World!
好
مرحبا أيها العالم! ! Привет мир!

A font that uses simple, smooth strokes, often of uniform thickness. For Latin scripts, they are identified by the lack of serifs (*sans* means *without*).

monospace

שלום העולם! Hello, World!

مرحبا أيها ال Привет мир!

A font in which all the characters in each script have the same width, like typewriter text.

cursive

Hello, World! *Hello, World!*

Hello, World! *Hello, World!*

A font that appears to be handwritten. It may be an elegant calligraphic script, a childish block print, or anything in between.

fantasy

HELLO, WORLD! Hello, World!

Hello, World! *Hello, World!*

A decorative or display font.

 The generic font name is a keyword, and should never be quoted.

In professional SVG work, using generic fonts may be acceptable for basic text labels on data visualizations or charts. Each operating system and browser renders fonts differently, and allowing the browser to pick the specific font usually results in clear and legible letters.

However, clear letters are only one part of legibility. The size and spacing of the glyphs can affect whether text overlaps other graphics, or fits within the dimensions of a button or border. Standard serif and sans-serif fonts can vary considerably from one to another in their effective size—how wide and tall the individual characters are relative to the font size—as well as their appearance. With the `cursive` and `fantasy` font classes, using generics means giving up control over the text appearance completely.

In addition, browsers are not currently very good at selecting an appropriate generic font for the script and language of the text. Most apply the same font family for all content, and fall back to their default font if the dedicated `serif` or `monospace` font family cannot display a given character.

For these reasons, in more complex graphical designs, the generic keywords are usually only used as fallbacks, after naming your prefered fonts.

Making the Most of System Fonts

Most web browsers have access to fonts on the user's computer, provided by the operating system or installed individually by the user. Names in the `font-family` list are searched against this database of installed system fonts. The match should be case insensitive, and should consider any language translations for font-family names provided in the font data.

 Font-family names may be quoted, but don't have to be—unless they contain a comma or other special character in the name!

With a little research and experimentation, you can sometimes create a list of font families that have similar appearance and dimensions and are collectively available on most common operating systems. This approach was used in the text-on-a-path examples (in Chapter 9) to select Times New Roman font or something like it:

```
text {
    font: bold italic 48px "Times New Roman", Times, serif;
}
```

 The `font-family` list is always the *last* part of the `font` shorthand. It *must* be preceded by the `font-size`. The `font-style` and `font-weight` modifier keywords at the beginning are optional.

If you want to ensure contrast between different fonts in a graphic, even if the exact font cannot be matched, make sure that the last value in each font-family list is a different generic keyword. These will always match an available font, and will nearly always be distinct from each other.

Once you go beyond the old reliable font families like Times or Arial/Helvetica, however, there are very few fonts that have close matches between operating systems. Because there are very many operating systems to consider, including mobile devices, using system fonts results in some unpredictability. In Example 5-4, which created a comic book effect for the text "BAM! BOOM!", we used the following font-family list:

```
font-family: "Gill Sans Ultra Bold",
             "Gill Sans", "Gill Sans MT",
             "Showcard Gothic",
             "Cooper Black", "Cooper",
             "Arial Black", "Arial",
             "Impact", sans-serif;
```

The first three values all reference the same font family under different names. The remaining families were selected because they include heavyweight, very emphatic typefaces. A font-weight of 900 was used to select the heaviest font face available in the family. However, the fonts are hardly interchangeable.

Figure 10-1 compares the same SVG code in our preferred font face (Gill Sans Ultra Bold), in the four fallback fonts, and finally in a *very* heavyweight decorative font (Goudy Stout). This last one was expressly left off the fallback list because "BAMBOO" does not have quite the same meaning as "BAM! BOOM!".

Beyond the difficulty of *finding* appropriate fallbacks for a decorative font, there is the question of whether your users will have it available. Even if the font is on the user's system, convincing a web browser to use it is not always easy.

To access font faces other than the usual regular, italic, and bold options, some browsers (Firefox) and operating systems will only match the simplified family name (e.g., "Gill Sans MT" or "Arial") while others (Internet Explorer and Chrome) will only match the extended family name (e.g., "Gill Sans Ultra Bold" or "Arial Black"). Chrome on Windows was unable to locate Gill Sans Ultra Bold from the system font folder under any name.

In addition, Firefox will match the PostScript name (e.g., "GillSans-UltraBold" or "Arial-Black"), which is always unique to a particular typeface, rather than describing a complete font family—but only within the local() source indicator of a font-face rule (which we'll get to in a moment!).

Including both versions of the font-family name, as done here, ensures the font will match if available. Unfortunately, according to the CSS font selection rules, a regular typeface from the font family will be used if it is available but the desired face is not, instead of using a similar face (ultra bold, condensed, etc.) from the next family in the fallback list. In other words, the text will be displayed in "Gill Sans MT" regular or bold, rather than in "Showcard Gothic" or "Cooper Black." Consider this carefully when designing your font stack, and decide whether the font family or the typeface parameters are most important.

As Figure 10-1 demonstrates, not only does the font affect the style and feeling of the text, it significantly affects the layout. The very *condensed* (narrow) Impact font takes up less than $2/_3$ of the width of the design, while the very *expanded* (wide) Goudy Stout stretches off the edge of the graphic. This is true despite the fact that all the text uses the same font size.

The layout in this particular graphic could be improved by using absolute x positioning instead of dx offsets. However, that isn't an option in most cases, where you want the letters to be spaced smoothly and naturally.

For these reasons, relying on the user's system fonts is rarely going to be your preferred choice for artistic SVG images.

Figure 10-1. The same SVG rendered with six different font families, as indicated: Gill Sans Ultra Bold, Showcard Gothic, Cooper Black, Arial Black, Impact, Goudy Stout

The Perfect Face

One of the most important aspects of SVG is that an SVG graphic is intended to be portable from one platform to the next. If the text is an artistic part of the graphic, most designers will expect it to have the same appearance whenever that graphic is displayed.

There are two distinct approaches to ensuring portability between systems. The first is to incorporate the font directly into the SVG itself. This provides the maximum degree of portability—in effect, the font is simply a set of reusable graphics, that are then drawn into the positions defined by the text.

Embedded fonts have been an option for PostScript files, including PDF, for decades. SVG was designed to have a similar facility, using the <font> and <glyph> elements among others. With these, you could declare the overall features and dimensions of the font as a whole and the specific shapes of individual letters and other glyphs.

SVG fonts allowed incredible flexibility, including multicolored letters, animation, and flexible coordinate systems; anything you could draw with SVG could be made into a font!

Unfortunately, as mentioned in Chapter 1, many browsers refused to support SVG fonts, and others have removed early implementations. SVG fonts therefore cannot be relied on to provide a consistent appearance on the Web.

Efforts are underway to redefine SVG fonts in a structure compatible with Open Type/Web Open Font Format. This would not change support for the use of SVG fonts included directly within the SVG markup. However, it will hopefully increase support for SVG fonts—in all their multicolored glory—by including them as CSS web fonts.

The alternative to embedding fonts is to provide the fonts by reference, as an external resource. The font is contained in a separate file on the web server (or a different server). The main document links to it similar to how it links to an external image file or stylesheet. These web-distributed font resources are known as web fonts to distinguish them from the system fonts installed on your computer.

Web fonts are supported in the SVG 1 fonts specification, which provided XML elements to specify the location of font files in various formats. Multiple files could be given so that a browser could choose a file in a supported format. This structure—defining a font's properties and the URL where it can be found—was designed to provide an XML parallel to the then-new web fonts syntax in CSS 2.

SVG fonts may have been poorly received, but CSS-based web fonts have become widely accepted. However, this is no "CSS versus SVG" issue: you can use the CSS font declarations in your SVG files. And although the CSS declarations usually link to external font files, they can also be used to embed font data in the form of a data URI.

A data URI provides a complete file in a format that is treated as a single URI/URL string for the purpose of the parent document. A data URI-encoded font cannot be easily edited like SVG font markup, but it does allow you to encapsulate all the data for your graphic within a single file. This can be useful if portability is essential. However, data URIs can significantly increase the file size, without any potential to cache the font for use in multiple pages or graphics on your website.

As external resources, web fonts will not be downloaded when they are referenced from an SVG used as an embedded image (an HTML `<img>` or CSS `background-image`).

Most browsers *will* use a font that is included as a data URI; Safari and related WebKit browsers will not.

Blink browsers will also use an external web font within an image if it declared in the CSS for *both* the SVG image file and the web page that embeds it.

If web fonts are important, use inline SVG or embed your SVG file as an `<object>`.

Web fonts are declared in CSS using an `@font-face` rule, which may be declared in a `<style>` element or an external stylesheet. The `@font-face` rule is properly called a *pragma*; it defines an entity (a particular font file and its properties) that can be used by the rest of the stylesheet. It does not set the value of a style property on any particular element.

Figure 10-2. An SVG that uses two custom fonts

In order to *use* a web font, you first describe its properties in the `@font-face` rule, and then set an element to use a font with those same properties. The descriptors within an `@font-face` rule therefore look much the same as property declarations for an element. Each face (italic, bold, condensed, etc.) of a font requires a separate `@font-face` rule with descriptors for the styles that it will match.

Example 10-1 uses two `@font-face` rules to specify a pair of fonts with a handwriting style, one cursive and one block-print, that are then used to create the graphic shown in Figure 10-2.

Example 10-1. Using web fonts in an SVG

```
<svg xmlns="http://www.w3.org/2000/svg" xml:lang="en"
    xmlns:xlink="http://www.w3.org/1999/xlink"
```

```
    width="4.3in" height="4.3in" viewBox="0 0 400 400">
    <title>Dear Pen Pal</title>
    <style type="text/css">
@font-face {
    font-family: "hand-writing";
    font-weight: normal;
    font-style: italic;
    src: local("Morado Marker"), local("morado-marker"),
        url("../Fonts/morado marker.woff") format("woff"),
        url("../Fonts/morado marker.ttf") format("truetype");
    /* Morado by Peter Wiegel
       Downloaded from: http://www.dafont.com/morado.font
    */
}
@font-face {
    font-family: hand-writing;
    src: local("CoolStory"), local("CoolStory Regular"),
        url("../Fonts/coolstory regular.woff") format("woff"),
        url("../Fonts/coolstory regular.ttf") format("truetype");
    /* Cool Story by Peter Olexa
       Downloaded from: http://www.dafont.com/coolstory.font
    */
}
svg {
    background-color: lightSkyBlue;
    border: solid thin;
    margin: 10px;

    font-family: "hand-writing", cursive;
    font-size: 36px;
}
    </style>
    <defs>
        <rect id="paper" width="300" height="350" rx="3"/>
    </defs>
    <g transform="translate(-5,50) rotate(-20) skewY(5)">
        <use xlink:href="#paper" transform="translate(-10,15)"
            fill="black" fill-opacity="0.3"/>
        <use xlink:href="#paper" fill="linen" stroke="bisque"/>
        <g transform="translate(0,20)">
            <text font-style="italic" font-size="48px"
                x="30" y="50" >Dear Pen Pal,</text>
            <text>
                <tspan x="10" y="100">Today, I received a</tspan>
                <tspan x="10" dy="50">new letter from my</tspan>
                <tspan x="10" dy="50">pen pal.  Hooray!</tspan>
            </text>
            <text font-style="italic" font-size="48px"
                x="100" y="250" >Sincerely,</text>
            <text x="200" y="300" font-size="larger">Me</text>
        </g>
```

```
    </g>
</svg>
```

The first line in each `@font-face` rule is a `font-family` description:

```
@font-face {
    font-family: "hand-writing";
```

This `font-family` descriptor is required. It declares the font-family name that will be used when matching the `font-family` settings of specific elements in the document. It does *not* have to be the normal name for that font; it could be a name that describes the specific way in which you are using the font. The name may be quoted—and should be if it has apostrophes, quotes, or commas in it—but it does not have to be.

Both font faces defined in Example 10-1 will be referenced by the family name `hand-writing`. Which typeface gets used depends on the other descriptors. The first face is declared to match normal-weight italic text:

```
font-weight: normal;
font-style: italic;
```

The second font-face rule does not have any `font-weight` or `font-style` descriptors. These are set to the default values: normal weight and normal style. As with the font-family name, these declared features do not have to match the features defined in the font file. In Example 10-1, a bold-weight, normal-style cursive writing font (Morado Marker) is used as the italic version of a block print handwriting font (Cool Story).

After the `@font-face` header has been parsed, the name given by the `font-family` description is the name by which the SVG graphic refers to the font in `font-family` properties of individual elements. The typeface name defined in the font file itself will not match.

When you use the fonts in style declarations, you should also give appropriate fallback fonts. In Example 10-1, the natural fallback was a generic `cursive` font:

```
font-family: "hand-writing", cursive;
```

The `font-family` style is applied to the entire `<svg>`. Because both of the font faces were declared to have the same family, the distinction comes from whether or not the text is given a `font-style` of `italic`. The font-style could be set using any of the ways in which

---

style properties are set. In Example 10-1, it is set using presentation attributes on individual <text> elements:

```
<text font-style="italic" font-size="48px"
      x="100" y="250" >Sincerely,</text>
```

The final descriptor in each @font-face rule, src, tells the browser where the font file is located:

```
src: local("Morado Marker"), local("morado-marker"),
     url("../Fonts/morado marker.woff") format("woff"),
     url("../Fonts/morado marker.ttf") format("truetype");
```

The src descriptor is also required—otherwise, there's no purpose to having the @font-face rule. It accepts a list of comma-separated options, in order of preference. There are two ways to specify the location:

- As the name of a font to look up on the user's system, wrapped in the local() function;
- As a URL to a location on the Web (absolute or relative), in a url() function, with an optional font format descriptor—wrapped in the format() function—so the browser knows whether it can use the file *before* it downloads it.

Within a single src list, the *first* value that the browser can match will be used, similar to the font-family list for an individual element. However, because the syntax for CSS fonts has changed since they were first introduced, you may see multiple src declarations, with the earlier versions not including format() or local(). In that case, the normal CSS error-handling and cascade rules apply: the *last* src list that is in a syntax the browser recognizes will be used.

In the case of local fonts, you may sometimes need to include a couple variants of the name to support equivalent fonts on different operating systems or in different file formats. However, only the US English version of the name should match.

 The requirement to use American English names is unique to local(). For historical reasons, system fonts specified in the font-family fallback list should match in any language.

Within a src declaration, local font names should always be listed first. Both you and your website's vistor will save bandwidth if a local version of the font is used when available, instead of downloading a web font file.

 When using local fonts, Blink browsers will synthesize italic or bold effects if there is a fontfamily name match but not a match for the specified typeface weight or style. In contrast, the same font file will not be modified if it is provided as a web font.

The font-synthesize property (not yet supported in Blink) will allow content authors to control whether or not *faux* bold or italic is allowed when styling text, but it is not specifically supported for local() font matches within an @font-face rule.

If there is no local match, the browser then examines the URL options, and in particular the information about font formats. The format() parameter src is an optional—but highly recommended—hinting mechanism. Browsers can determine the font type from the MIME type in the file header, but because similar fonts don't always have unique MIME types, the format() statement provides an additional hint. More importantly, if a font can be identified by type, the browser doesn't need to request and start downloading all of the fonts listed before finding one that it can work with.

Many different font formats are available as web fonts, but not all browsers support all formats equally. For most modern browsers, you want the WOFF or WOFF2 formats. (If you are going to embed a font as a data URI, WOFF is currently your best bet for size and support.) For older browsers, you might need TrueType/OpenType, Microsoft's proprietary Embedded OpenType, or even SVG fonts, which were the only web font supported on early iPhones.

The Web Open Font Format, `format("woff")`, is a font format standardized by the W3C Web Fonts Working Group. The format is essentially a modified OpenType or TrueType Font that makes use of a compression scheme to reduce the overall size of such fonts by 50%–60%. Because font download times can be significant —it is not uncommon for some larger fonts to run upward of several megabytes in size—this compression scheme is essential for website performance.

The specification for the WOFF 2.0 font format, with even better compression, has not been finalized at the time of writing. Indicated in CSS by `format("woff2")`, it is already supported in the latest Blink and Firefox browsers.

If it is vital to your design that your chosen font is used on any device, you can take advantage of numerous font conversion tools to provide your font in legacy formats. Be sure to present the different sources in the correct order—the *first* value in the *last* `src` descriptor is the preferred option:

```
@font-face {
    font-family: "MyFont";

    /* IE9 Compatible */
    src: url("my_font.eot");

    /* Modern Syntax */
            /* Try local first */
    src: local("My Font"), local("MyFont"),
            /* the latest browsers */
        url("my_font.woff2") format("woff2"),
            /* most modern browsers */
        url("my_font.woff") format("woff"),
            /* older Safari, Android, iOS */
        url("my_font.ttf") format("truetype"),
            /* oldest iOS */
        url("my_font.svgz") format("svg");
}
```

Nonetheless, be aware that some browser settings may still prevent the download of web fonts, regardless of formats. In particular, the Opera Mini browser—which is designed for affordable mobile phones on expensive mobile networks—never downloads web fonts.

Finding Fonts

`@font-face` has a long and somewhat troubled history. The idea that web pages should be able to set fonts in the same way as word-processing software has been around practically from the earliest days of the Web. However, typeface files—which take dozens to hundreds of hours to create—typically have been closely guarded by the font foundries.

Putting a font onto the Web meant that such fonts could be grabbed for free. Needless to say, this did not sit well with the various foundries. There have consequently been a number of different schemes for trying to protect these fonts, including proposals within versions of the CSS Fonts specifications.

In practice, what has happened is much the same as happened in most other media areas: the combination of large numbers of font producers (many of them working as amateurs or producing fonts that they initially developed as part of other projects) and the availability of file sharing essentially rendered the point moot. Like clip-art and icons, there are many sources of free fonts and many more sources of paid ones. Some of these services also host the font files on their own web servers.

The free fonts tend to lean toward decorative fonts that cover limited scripts and only look good when drawn large—but that is often all you need for SVG. Web fonts used in this book were either downloaded from DaFont.com (*http://www.dafont.com/*) (a database of free and shareware fonts with various licence restrictions) or are imported from Google Fonts (*https://www.google.com/fonts*) (completely free web fonts).

When considering a web font, be sure the licence—whether free or paid—allows you to *distribute* the font. Even if you have the right to unlimited commercial use of the font, that only applies to using the font to create print products, not making the font itself available on your website.

For no-restriction web fonts, look for fonts released under the SIL Open Font Licence.

As web fonts have become popular, a new controversy has arisen. Fonts are not small files. As more web fonts are available, and more websites use them, fonts have started to compete with raster images as one of the largest contributors to website downloads. The two fonts used in Example 10-1 add up to nearly 50KB if the compressed WOFF files are used, and more than 90KB for the uncompressed TrueType files. Unless you're using those same font files throughout your website, that cancels out the file size benefits of using SVG.

Theoretically, a document can load any number of fonts via the @font-face mechanism, but performance considerations should drive you to use fonts sparingly. Font downloads not only cost your users in bandwidth, they can effectively block out users on slower connections.

Font-loading takes time. In some browsers, it is an asynchronous operation: the SVG graphic will render the text with the first available font given in a font-family list, and if a more appropriate one loads afterward, the browser will redraw. The user may be confused or disoriented from seeing a block of text styled one way transform suddenly into a different look. Other browsers avoid this "flash of unstyled text" by not drawing anything at all while waiting for a font download—but that just creates a "flash of invisible text," making the site unusable while waiting for large downloads.

For certain graphics, such as company logos, you can address the size and therefore the speed by *subsetting* the font to only contain the characters you will use. There are various programs that process a font to create a subset, or if you're using the Google Fonts API you can include the characters in your font request; some paid font subscriptions offer similar options.

If you're embedding the font as a data URI in your SVG file, you will almost always want to subset it to only include the necessary characters. Embedding a subset font should *not* be done if the same font is used in many documents or graphics on the website, as you lose the benefit of having a single asset file that can be used by all documents.

If using one of the most popular Google Fonts (such as Open Sans, used by Google itself), avoid creating a custom subset. The browser likely has already cached the font from another website.

Once a web font is downloaded, it is cached just like an image or script. This means that if you plan to display an SVG graphic that makes extensive use of fonts you expect will have to be downloaded —such as a complex data visualizations or maps—it may be worth-while to include the same font declarations (with the exact same `src` files) in a placeholder loading graphic. That way, the fonts will start downloading while waiting for the more complex SVG to load.

There is one last restriction on using web fonts that can cause head-aches if you aren't aware of it. Fonts are binary resources that are interpreted, and as with any code that can execute content, they can launch viruses or other code nasties. For this reason, web fonts are subject to the same cross-origin restrictions as files accessed by scripts. If the font file URL is not on the same web server—and accessed by the same HTTP protocol—as your document, it must be served with cross-origin headers that explicitly allow your web domain to use it.

The security benefit may be questionable (font files are unlikely to contain personal data), but cross-origin restrictions provide extra copyright control for the many paid-subscription web font servers. Each subscribing website accesses the font with a URL that will return HTTP headers allowing its use on that specific web domain. In contrast, Google's free font servers use headers that allow the files to be accessed from any domain.

Faking Fonts

With all the complications of getting fonts to work as expected on the Web, one option popular with designers is to replace the text with SVG shapes. The main graphical editing programs (e.g., Illus-trator, Inkscape) include an option for converting text to path— effectively "printing" text to a predictable graphical representation, by generating shapes of the individual letters' outlines in your chosen font.

Creating paths from text effectively subsets and embeds the font, avoiding any rendering problems if the user does not have access to the same font. It also circumvents many licencing restrictions: because you're not distributing complete font files, any font that you have the right to use in print publications can be used as a text-to-path representation.

For all these reasons—and because it is well supported by graphics programs, but embedded CSS web fonts are not—converting text to path is still popular for logos and advertisements where consistent font rendering is considered essential.

However, converting text to shapes removes all the meaning associated with the text. It cannot be easily edited and no longer makes sense to search engines or screen readers. If you use this technique, be sure to include equivalent, machine-readable text. Unfortunately, most graphics tools will not do this automatically.

There are two options for including readable text in addition to the text-to-path shapes:

- Use a `<title>` or `<desc>` element, or `aria-label` attribute, in inline SVG, or an `alt` attribute on the HTML image that embeds it. The latest versions of Inkscape use an `aria-label` attribute to preserve text content for screen readers when converting text to path.

- Include `<text>` elements in the SVG that draw transparent letters (in a generic font) over top of the visible shapes.

The invisible `<text>` elements have the benefit of making the text available not only to accessibility technologies but also to regular users trying to select it (e.g., to copy it into a search engine or translation software). To make the invisible text interactive, you will need to set the `pointer-events` property to `painted` so that the text can be selected even when its `opacity` is 0. For best results, you'll also want to make sure the size and spacing of the generic font text is adjusted to match your custom font, using the methods that we'll discuss in Chapter 11.

The Perfect Fit

If you cannot always control the font the browser uses, even with web fonts, what can you do to ensure that your overall text layout is preserved?

There are two ways you can hint to the browser how much space a given text element should take up. One comes from CSS, and adjusts the used font size. The other is SVG specific, and adjusts the spacing and width of the letters. Surprisingly, it is the CSS option that has the poorer browser support, although neither is as reliable as one would like.

Fixing Font Size

To reemphasize *why* text size control is important, consider Figure 11-1. It shows the SVG from Figure 10-2, and then the exact same SVG code displayed using a fallback `cursive` font (Comic Sans MS) instead of the chosen web fonts. The font itself doesn't have the fun and artistic feel of the web fonts, but it is the sizing that really creates the problem. The floating letters running off the page significantly distract from the appearance of writing on paper, don't you think?

Part of the problem is that the lowercase letters in Comic Sans take up a much larger proportion of the height; in other words, their ex-height is larger for the same em-height. The letters are correspondingly wider, despite the same `font-size`. This is a common source of inconsistency in text sizing when changing between font families.

Figure 11-1. An SVG designed for two custom fonts: rendered with the intended fonts (left) and rendered with a fallback font (right)

The ex-height to em-height ratio is often known as the aspect ratio or aspect value of a font, although it does not directly correspond to the width to height ratio.

The problem is so common, even with non-graphical text layouts, that CSS 2 introduced the `font-size-adjust` property. Its value is a number (usually between 0.4 and 0.6) that represents the ex-height to em-height ratio of your *preferred* font. If the browser is using a font with a different aspect ratio, it is supposed to adjust the used font size so that the *ex*-height remains constant, instead of the em-height.

Unfortunately, browser uptake was poor. At the time of writing, Firefox is the only major browser that implements `font-size-adjust`. It was removed from the core CSS 2.1 specification in favor of including it within CSS 3 Fonts.

One of the main problems with `font-size-adjust` is that it can be difficult to calculate the correct aspect ratio. Font files do not always explicitly state the ex-height value, and different browsers use different tools to estimate it.

For any given browser (which at this point means, for Firefox), the best way to determine the aspect ratio of a font is to create a sample page in that font. Then, incrementally change the `font-size-`

adjust value until the displayed text size matches the size when font-size-adjust is left as the default none.

You can use a :hover or :focus pseudoclass selector rule to reset font-size-adjust to none, allowing you to quickly switch back and forth between the normal and adjusted size, to see if there is a change.

Adjusting the font size addresses the apparent size and legibility of individual letters, but it does not directly alter the layout impact from the width of the letters. The SVG textLength attribute fills this need. It specifies exactly how long the text should be, in your chosen font. The browser should adjust the displayed text to match.

textLength is an XML attribute, not a presentation attribute. It cannot be set using CSS.

The specifications allow textLength to be specified either for the <text> as a whole or for an individual <tspan>, but this is not well supported in browsers:

Blink/WebKit browsers do not adjust content within a <tspan> or <textPath> based on the textLength for a parent <text> element.

Firefox does not respond to textLength on a <tspan> or <textPath>, only on <text>.

Internet Explorer can handle constraints on any text element, but is very erratic—with sudden shifts in layout as the user interacts with the graphic—if there are lengths set on *both* the <text> and the child <tspan> or <textPath>.

In other words, for consistent results in current browsers, only use textLength on individual <text> elements without child <tspan> or <textPath> elements.

Example 11-1 integrates both these features into the pen-pal letter SVG from Example 10-1. The multiline text has been broken into separate absolutely positioned <text> elements each with a textLength attribute. The font sizes are standardized with font-size-adjust. Figure 11-2 shows the resulting layout, with or without web fonts, and with or without support for font-size-adjust.

Example 11-1. Using text sizing hints to control fallback fonts

```
<svg xmlns="http://www.w3.org/2000/svg" xml:lang="en"
    xmlns:xlink="http://www.w3.org/1999/xlink"
    width="4.3in" height="4.3in" viewBox="0 0 400 400">
    <title>Dear Pen Pal</title>
    <style type="text/css">
@font-face {                                                    ❶
    font-family: "hand-writing";
    font-weight: normal;
    font-style: italic;
    src: /* local("Morado Marker"), local("morado-marker"), */
        url("../Fonts/morado marker.woff") format("woff"),
        url("../Fonts/morado marker.ttf") format("truetype");
    /* Morado by Peter Wiegel
       Downloaded from: http://www.dafont.com/morado.font
    */
}
@font-face {
    font-family: hand-writing;
    src: local("CoolStory"), local("CoolStory Regular"),
        url("../Fonts/coolstory regular.woff") format("woff"),
        url("../Fonts/coolstory regular.ttf") format("truetype");
    /* CoolStory by Peter Olexa
       Downloaded from: http://www.dafont.com/coolstory.font
    */
}
svg {
    background-color: lightSkyBlue;
    border: solid thin;
    margin: 10px;

    font-family: "hand-writing", cursive;
    font-size: 36px;
    font-size-adjust: 0.50;                                     ❷

}
    </style>
    <defs>
        <rect id="paper" width="300" height="350" rx="3"/>
    </defs>
```

```
<g transform="translate(-5,50) rotate(-20) skewY(5)">
    <use xlink:href="#paper" transform="translate(-10,15)"
        fill="black" fill-opacity="0.3"/>
    <use xlink:href="#paper" fill="linen" stroke="bisque"/>
    <g transform="translate(0,20)">
        <text font-style="italic"
            x="30" y="50" >Dear Pen Pal,</text>          ❸
        <text x="10" y="100" textLength="245"
            >Today, I received a</text>                   ❹
        <text x="10" y="150" textLength="260"
            >new letter from my</text>
        <text x="10" y="200" textLength="200"
            >pen pal.  Hooray!</text>
        <text font-style="italic"
            x="100" y="250" >Sincerely,</text>
        <text x="200" y="300" font-size="larger">Me</text>
    </g>
</g>
</svg>
```

❶ The @font-face rules have not changed.

❷ The font-size-adjust value was determined empirically in
   Firefox to be the value that did *not* cause adjustments in the preferred web font.

❸ The "italic" font used in the greeting and signature line no
   longer has a separate font-size presentation attribute. Instead,
   it will be scaled with font-size-adjust to match the rest of
   the text.

❹ Each of the full-width text lines is given its own textLength
   value. Again, the values were determined empirically, by finding
   the value that did *not* change the text length when the preferred
   font was used.

Although the fallback versions in Figure 11-2 are not as artistic as
the web font versions, the overall layout is preserved. Without font-
size-adjust, the cramped letters make it slightly difficult to read,
but it is acceptable.

The biggest remaining problem with the layout occurs when the
web fonts *are* used, but font-size-adjust is not. Although the two
web fonts had a similar overall look, they have extremely different
aspect ratios, and so look mismatched when they are set with the
same font size. Even with font-size-adjust, the resulting size

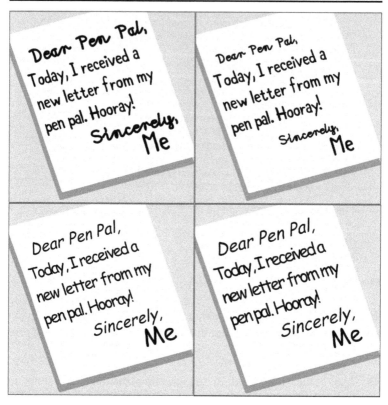

Figure 11-2. An SVG that uses custom fonts and size adjustments, in various fallback scenarios: with the chosen web fonts (top row); with Comic Sans MS fallback font (bottom row); in a browser that supports font-size-adjust (left side), without font-size-adjust (right side)

doesn't match the size used in the original graphic (compare with Figure 11-1), when the font size was adjusted manually.

It would have been better to set them as completely different fonts, with different font sizes and font-size-adjust values. However, we would then need to also give them textLength values to cancel out the effect of the larger font size on the fallback fonts when font-size-adjust is not supported.

Given these examples, a few guidelines can be established, based on current browser support:

- Use `textLength` whenever too-long or too-short text will significantly throw off the layout, but only if the text can be laid out as individual `<text>` elements.

- Consider using `font-size-adjust` to minimize the amount of layout squeezing or stretching that the browser has to do to match the `textLength`.

- Do not rely on `font-size-adjust` to synchronize the sizes of very different fonts.

- Do not create composite font families (like the mismatched `hand-writing` family used here) unless the individual font faces have very similar dimensions at the same `font-size` setting.

Although `font-size-adjust` cannot be relied on except for small, optional adjustments, `textLength` is essential for many SVG layouts. However, manually determining the length for each span through trial and error can be a hassle. Fortunately, it is also not necessary.

Measuring SVG Text

Every SVG element has a corresponding object within the document object model (DOM) created by a web browser parsing your markup. These DOM objects can be created, deleted, or modified by scripts running in the browser.

All SVG elements can be manipulated by the core DOM methods defined for all XML and HTML documents. However, the SVG specifications also define their own DOM interfaces for each element type, with properties and methods to make it easier to geometrically manipulate graphics.

SVG text elements, in particular, have methods for determining the position and angle of individual letters and the amount of space consumed by the text. The `getComputedTextLength()` method returns the total length of an element's text content in the text direction. It includes any letter or word spacing or internal offsets from dx and dy attributes, and uses the font metrics of the element as it is currently displayed. This is the exact same computation used for the `textLength` attribute: if the two lengths match, no adjustment is applied.

As a result, to find out which values you should use in your `textLength` attributes, open your SVG in a browser that displays it just the way you want. Use the developer's console (which can usually be accessed with the F12 key) to select all the `<text>`, `<tspan>`, and `<textPath>` elements, and then print out the computed text length for each. Copying and pasting the following code should do the trick:

```
var texts = document.querySelectorAll("text, tspan, textPath");
for(var i=0, n=texts.length; i<n; i++) {
    console.log(texts[i].getComputedTextLength(),
                texts[i].tagName,
                texts[i].textContent.slice(0,8));
}
```

Each element's length will be printed out along with the type of tag and the first few letters (so you can figure out which one's which). The computed values do *not* include any adjustments from `textLength` attributes.

When run in an HTML document, the preceding snippet will not select `<textPath>` elements in older WebKit and Blink browsers, as their selector-matching algorithm would automatically lowercase all selectors, but would not automatically lowercase SVG tag names. As mentioned in Chapter 9, the latest browser versions have implemented workarounds, treating SVG tag names as case insensitive in HTML.

For the original pen-pal letter (Example 10-1, with nested `<tspan>` elements and without any `font-size-adjust` changes), the code prints out the following values in Firefox:

```
235.9729461669922 "text" "Dear Pen"
737.9719848632812 "text" "         "
248.21682739257812 "tspan" "Today, I"
261.57379150390625 "tspan" "new lett"
210.3721160888672 "tspan" "pen pal."
171.97085571289062 "text" "Sincerel"
53.984378814697266 "text" "Me"
```

In other browsers, the exact values will be slightly different even with the same fonts and font sizes, because of differences in the text layout algorithms used. However, they should be fairly close. These values are also close to the ones used in Example 11-1: 248 versus 245 for the line starting "Today," 261.5 versus 260 for the span starting "new letter." In other words, you can round the values off without having a noticeable impact.

The `getComputedTextLength()` function is only one of many SVG-specific DOM methods available to help you calculate layouts. Although for `textLength` it is used to determine a value that is then hard coded in the SVG markup, these methods are in general most useful when using JavaScript to create dynamic SVG layouts based on changing data.

Fun with Font Adjustments

Although *intended* to be used to control browser and font differences in text layout, the `textLength` attribute can also be used for graphical effect. By setting `textLayout` to a value significantly different from the natural length of the text, you can force the browser to stretch or compress the text.

 Internet Explorer does not correctly apply `text-anchor` values other than `start` when the length of the text is constrained with `textLength`: the text is positioned based on its default length, not its adjusted length, so the result is misaligned.

Also keep in mind that some older browsers and other tools do not support `textLength` at all.

By default, the adjustments to text length are made by changing the spacing between letters evenly throughout the text (but not at the start or end of the string). Text length adjustments can therefore be a good substitute for `letter-spacing` and `word-spacing` in Firefox—although you won't be able to control how much of the extra spacing is positioned between letters versus between words.

However, for graphical effect, one of the most popular choices is to stretch or compress the letters themselves. This is done by setting the `lengthAdjust` attribute to `spacingAndGlyphs`, versus the default value `spacing`.

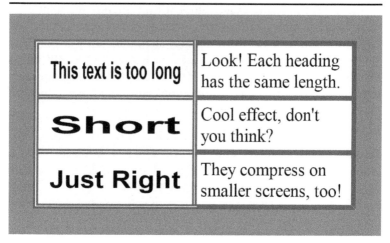

This text is too long	Look! Each heading has the same length.
Short	Cool effect, don't you think?
Just Right	They compress on smaller screens, too!

Figure 11-3. A web page that uses SVG text with adjusted lengths to balance heading widths

Again, `lengthAdjust` is an XML attribute, not a style property. The `spacingAndGlyphs` value must be explicitly set on every element with a `textLength` attribute.

Example 11-2 uses SVG to draw HTML table headings that are stretched or compressed to the same length. Figure 11-3 shows the final web page.

Example 11-2. Using textLength and lengthAdjust to stretch or compress text to a fixed length

```
<!DOCTYPE html>
<html lang="en">
<head>
    <meta charset="utf-8"/>
    <title>SVG lengthAdjust for Graphical Effect</title>
    <style>
        body {
            font: large serif;
            padding: 1em;
            background: lightSlateGray;
        }
        table {
            table-layout: fixed;
            border-collapse: collapse;
```

```
            background: white;
            width: 100%;
        }
        th, td {
            border: solid thick dimgray;
        }
        th {
            font: bold x-large sans-serif;
            background-color: #EEF;
            border-style: double;
            color: #222;
        }
        th svg {
            display: block;
            height: 1.25em;
            width: 100%;
            max-width: 12em;
            margin: auto;
            padding: 0.25em 0;
            overflow: visible;              ❶
        }
        th svg text {
            fill: currentColor;
            font-size: 24px;                ❷
        }
        td {
            padding: 0.2em;
        }
    </style>
</head>
<body>
    <table>
        <tr>
            <th><svg viewBox="0 0 135 30">         ❸
                <text dy="1em" textLength="135"
                    lengthAdjust="spacingAndGlyphs"
                    >This text is too long</text>     ❹
            </svg></th>
            <td>Look! Each heading has the
                same length.</td>
        </tr>
        <tr>
            <th><svg viewBox="0 0 135 30">
                <text dy="1em" textLength="135"
                    lengthAdjust="spacingAndGlyphs"
                    >Short</text>                     ❺
            </svg></th>
            <td>Cool effect, don't you think?</td>
        </tr>
        <tr>
            <th><svg viewBox="0 0 135 30">
```

```
            <text dy="1em" textLength="135"
                  lengthAdjust="spacingAndGlyphs"
                  >Just Right</text>
        </svg></th>
        <td>They compress on smaller screens, too!</td>
      </tr>
    </table>
  </body>
</html>
```

❶ The styles on each <svg> control its size to fit within the table. It fills the full width of the cell if necessary, but no more than 1.25em height (in the x-large font size set on the <th>). The SVGs' scaled viewBox will fit into this size, centered in the available space, using the default xMidYMid meet value for preserveAspectRatio.

❷ The text uses the color set in the table heading (<th>) element. The 24px font-size value will be interpreted within the scaled SVG coordinate system.

❸ The viewBox fits 30 units within the height of the SVG. At an internal font size of 24px, that's 1.25em. Because the SVG was also set to a height of 1.25em, the result is that the text will scale to match the x-large value set in the table. Which happens to be equal to 24px in my browsers, but might be different in yours. The SVG coordinate system—and therefore the text—will scale down if the SVG becomes too narrow for the viewBox aspect ratio.

❹ The text element is positioned vertically in the space with dy, but starts at x="0" by default. The textLength attribute sets it to fill the full width declared in the viewBox, while lengthAdjust tells the browser to stretch the glyphs as required to make the text fit.

❺ The other headings use the exact same attributes on the <svg> and <text> elements.

The SVG includes a viewBox so the text will scale down (in both directions) when there is not enough room. Unfortunately, textLength alone cannot achieve the same effect: the textLength

---

property cannot be expressed as a percentage of the coordinate system, only as a length (with units or as a number of user units).

This example again emphasizes how SVG text can be used within HTML to create short stretches of decorative text. However, there are also many text layouts that are easy with HTML (and basic CSS layout) but not SVG. For diagrams and data visualizations with a lot of text, it would be nice to use this HTML formatting within your SVG graphic. Chapter 12 describes how.

Extending Your Toolbox

SVG text, as we've mentioned a few times already, is designed for incredibly detailed control of layout, but at the cost of little support for automated multiline text blocks. That was quickly identified as its main weakness; SVG's support for flowing, multiline text was dramatically strengthened in the proposed SVG 1.2 specification, but even the changes in the completed 1.2 Tiny specification were not significantly adopted by browsers. Until SVG 2 support is widespread, the SVG `<text>` element is restricted to manually positioned text lines.

However, this does not mean that SVG *cannot* include multiline flowing text—it only means that to do so, it needs to make use of a `<foreignObject>` element and render HTML within the SVG context.

A Foreigner in an SVG File

The `<foreignObject>` element can be seen as a type of portal or escape hatch, shifting the document out of the realm of SVG layout and into any other XML layout mode supported by the browser. Two types of XML content were in particular considered when the SVG specifications were created: XHTML and MathML.

Internet Explorer never supported the `<foreignObject>` element, although it has been implemented for Microsoft Edge.

There are a number of bugs and inconsistencies in other browsers' implementations, so be sure to test thoroughly.

It is solely within the purview of the browser as to what types of content *can* be rendered. Web-browser SVG implementations can usually render basic HTML, but other SVG environments may not support it. MathML—which defines mathematical equations and could be very useful for annotating a technical diagram—is not currently supported in web browsers other than Firefox; however, it could be useful for SVG within a textbook if you have full control over the software that will render the graphic.

Although `<foreignObject>` can render any content recognized by the browser, most of the time it's used to add paragraphs of HTML text within a rectangular region. This is analogous to how the `<svg>` element in HTML 5 defines a region in that page for drawing a vector graphic.

The `<foreignObject>` element itself is positioned using x, y, width and height attributes, similar to an `<image>`. The child content is then drawn within this space as if that was the browser window or `<iframe>`.

The type of foreign content is identified by its XML namespace. In this case, that's `"http://www.w3.org/1999/xhtml"` for XML-compatible HTML.

Example 12-1 uses `<foreignObject>` elements to include blocks of descriptive text to a legend of all the SVG shape elements. Not only does the text wrap automatically, but the paragraphs scroll if required. Figure 12-1 shows a screenshot of the page as it appears in the browser.

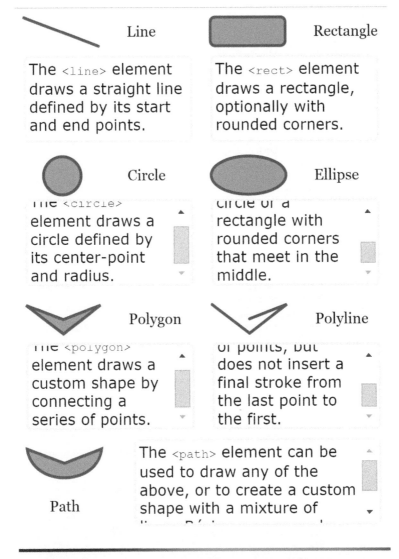

Figure 12-1. An SVG diagram with HTML content embedded using foreignObject

Example 12-1. Using foreign objects to include multiline, scrollable text in SVG

```
<svg xmlns="http://www.w3.org/2000/svg" xml:lang="en"
     width="4in" height="6.5in" viewBox="0 0 400 650" >
    <title>ForeignObjects describing SVG Shapes</title>
    <style type="text/css">
        @namespace html "http://www.w3.org/1999/xhtml";    ❶
        .shape {
            fill: deepSkyBlue;                             ❷
            stroke: blueViolet;
            stroke-width: 3px;
            stroke-linecap: round;
        }
        .backdrop {
            fill: #CED;
        }
        text {
            font-size: medium;
            font-family: serif;
        }
        text[role="heading"] {
            font: bold 64px sans-serif;
            text-decoration: underline overline;
            white-space: pre;
            fill: url(#blue-shine) darkBlue;
        }
        html|* {
            box-sizing: border-box;                        ❸
        }
        html {
            height: 100%;                                  ❹
            width: 100%;
            background-color: white;
            border: 2px solid lightGray;
            border-radius: 5px;
            overflow: auto;                                ❺
        }
        p {
            font-family: sans-serif;                       ❻
            width: 100%;
            height: 100%;
            margin: 0;
            padding: 0.1em 0.2em;
        }
    </style>
    <linearGradient id="blue-shine" y2="100%">
        <stop offset="0.1" stop-color="darkBlue" />
        <stop offset="0.3" stop-color="deepSkyBlue" />
        <stop offset="0.5" stop-color="dodgerBlue" />
        <stop offset="0.7" stop-color="darkBlue" />
```

```
</linearGradient>
<rect width="100%" height="100%" class="backdrop" />
<g>
    <line x1="10" y1="10" x2="90" y2="40" class="shape" />
    <text x="120" y="30" >Line</text>
    <foreignObject x="10" y="50" width="180" height="90"> ❺
        <html xmlns="http://www.w3.org/1999/xhtml"
                tabindex="0">                           ❻
            <p>The <code>&lt;line&gt;</code> element draws
                a straight line defined by its start and
                end points.</p>                          ❼
        </html>
    </foreignObject>
</g>
<g transform="translate(200,0)">
    <rect x="10" y="10" width="80" height="30" rx="5"
            class="shape" />
    <text x="120" y="30" >Rectangle</text>
    <foreignObject x="10" y="50" width="180" height="90"> ❽
        <html xmlns="http://www.w3.org/1999/xhtml"
                tabindex="0">
            <p>The <code>&lt;rect&gt;</code> element draws
                a rectangle, optionally with rounded
                corners.</p>
        </html>
    </foreignObject>
</g>
<g transform="translate(0,150)">
    <circle cx="50" cy="25" r="20" class="shape" />
    <text x="120" y="30" >Circle</text>
    <foreignObject x="10" y="50" width="180" height="90">
        <html xmlns="http://www.w3.org/1999/xhtml"
                tabindex="0">
            <p>The <code>&lt;circle&gt;</code> element draws
                a circle defined by its center-point and
                radius.</p>
        </html>
    </foreignObject>
</g>
<g transform="translate(200,150)">
    <ellipse cx="50" cy="25" rx="40" ry="20" class="shape" />
    <text x="120" y="30" >Ellipse</text>
    <foreignObject x="10" y="50" width="180" height="90">
        <html xmlns="http://www.w3.org/1999/xhtml"
                tabindex="0">
            <p>The <code>&lt;ellipse&gt;</code> element draws
                an ellipse, which is like a stretched circle
                or a rectangle with rounded corners that meet
                in the middle.</p>
        </html>
    </foreignObject>
```

```
        </g>
        <g transform="translate(0,300)">
            <polygon points="10,10 50,40 90,10 50,25" class="shape" />
            <text x="120" y="30" >Polygon</text>
            <foreignObject x="10" y="50" width="180" height="90">
                <html xmlns="http://www.w3.org/1999/xhtml"
                        tabindex="0">
                    <p>The <code>&lt;polygon&gt;</code> element draws
                        a custom shape by connecting a series of
                        points.</p>
                </html>
            </foreignObject>
        </g>
        <g transform="translate(200,300)">
            <polyline points="10,10 50,40 90,10 50,25"
                        class="shape" style="fill: none" />
            <text x="120" y="30" >Polyline</text>
            <foreignObject x="10" y="50" width="180" height="90">
                <html xmlns="http://www.w3.org/1999/xhtml"
                        tabindex="0">
                    <p>The <code>&lt;polyline&gt;</code> element
                        also connects a series of points,
                        but does not insert a final stroke from the
                        last point to the first.</p>
                </html>
            </foreignObject>
        </g>
        <g transform="translate(0,450)">
            <path d="M10,10 C15,50 85,50 90,10 L50,25 Z" class="shape" />
            <text x="50" y="75" text-anchor="middle">Path</text>
            <foreignObject x="125" y="0" width="265" height="90">
                <html xmlns="http://www.w3.org/1999/xhtml"
                        tabindex="0">
                    <p>The <code>&lt;path&gt;</code> element
                        can be used to draw any of the above,
                        or to create a custom shape with a mixture
                        of lines, Bézier curves, and arcs.</p>
                </html>
            </foreignObject>
        </g>
        <text x="50%" text-anchor="middle" transform="translate(0,625)"
            textLength="400" lengthAdjust="spacingAndGlyphs"
            xml:space="preserve"
            role="heading"> SVG Shapes </text>
</svg>
```

❶ An @namespace declaration at the top of the <style> block defines a prefix by which style rules may specifically target XHTML elements.

❷ The SVG styles should be familiar by now; the text labels are quite basic, but a heading takes advantage of a number of styling features, including a gradient fill, preserved whitespace, and an adjusted text length.

❸ To make it easier to size the HTML elements precisely without clipping, box-sizing is set to border-box on all elements in the HTML namespace. Considering that box-sizing does not have an effect on SVG elements, the namespace is optional—but it's a reminder that you can use XML namespaces in CSS selectors!

❹ To make the HTML content fill up the entire space allotted to it, a height of 100% is set explicitly on each <html> element. Background and border styles decorate the box.

❺ The overflow property ensures that the paragraph will be scrollable if the content exceeds the set height.

❻ The <p> paragraph elements are likewise styled using all the properties you can use in an HTML document.

❼ In the markup, each <foreignObject> element is positioned and sized using x, y, width, and height.

❽ The foreign content needs to be a valid XML document fragment, and is identified by the xmlns attribute on an <html> element.)))Because these elements may need to be scrolled by the user, they have a tabindex attribute to ensure that keyboard users can access them.

❾ Within the HTML-namespaced content, you can use any HTML elements as usual, and the browser's default styling will apply—such as monospaced font for <code> elements. Note, however, that you still cannot use HTML-specific entities, which cause XML validation errors before the browser even parses the markup. The < and > entities used here are defined for all XML.

❿ The other <foreignObject> elements are similar, each one positioned within the transformed coordinate system created by the <g> elements.

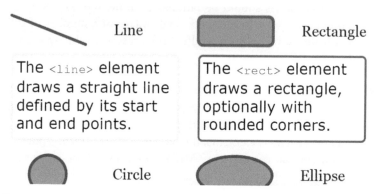

Figure 12-2. Partial screenshot of the SVG with HTML content, showing hover effects

Because the `<foreignObject>` is positioned within the local SVG coordinate system, it is affected by all transformations including rotations, skews, and scaling effects. The foreign object can also be affected by any graphical effects that can apply to a grouping element, such as masks and clipping.

Although the foreign HTML content is laid out as if it was in an `<iframe>`, it is still part of the same document. Just as with inline SVG in an HTML document, this means that the same style rules apply to both types of content. So, for example, you can add a hover/focus effect with rules like the following:

```
g:hover html, html:focus {
    border-color: crimson;
}
g:hover .shape {
    stroke: crimson;
}
```

If *either* the text or the graphics are moused-over, the parent `<g>` element will match the `:hover` pseudoclass, and both types of content will be highlighted to emphasize their connection. Figure 12-2 shows the relevant part of the graphic when the rectangle description is hovered.

Making the effect keyboard accessible is more difficult, however. The `:focus` pseudoclass only applies on the directly focused element, not its ancestors. You *could* add `tabindex="0"` and `focusable="true"` attributes to each `<g>` to make them focusable in most browsers. However, to allow users to scroll the text elements, it is the <html> elements that should be keyboard focusable. The new :has(*selector*) pseudoclass selector (introduced by the Selectors Level 4 specification) will address this difficulty, allowing you to style the SVG graphics with the following rule:

```
g:has(:focus) .shape {
    stroke: crimson;
}
```

Unfortunately, :has() is not currently supported in web browsers. What's worse, unrecognized selectors in CSS invalidate an entire rule, so you cannot simply add the future-focused syntax as a comma-separated alternative after the :hover selector. Instead, the entire rule needs to be duplicated with the new syntax.

Another potential use of <foreignObject> and HTML is to integrate form input elements and other interactive content within your graphic, allowing you to make use of all the native functionality of these elements in HTML. However, this is one area where implementations are currently very buggy. The appearance of input elements may not be correctly updated when the user interacts with them.

 Although you can apply many SVG effects to foreign content, a <foreignObject> cannot be duplicated with <use>; one reason for that restriction is to avoid multiple conflicting instances of the same input element.

When SVG is inline in an HTML 5 page, limited support for (and bugs within) <foreignObject> can sometimes be patched-over by simply making it *appear* that the HTML content is contained inside your SVG. Sibling HTML and SVG elements can be positioned on the same region of the page by including the <svg> and the HTML elements within a wrapper <div> or <figure>, and using CSS absolute positioning to place the HTML content. SVG graphical effects do not apply to the superimposed HTML content, but with increasing support for transformations and masks in HTML, that is less of an issue; many of the effects you would want to apply to a block of embedded text can be applied to the HTML elements directly.

Even as more graphical effects are being adopted into HTML, the need to embed foreign-namespaced text content in SVG should diminish. With multiline text support in SVG 2, HTML `<foreignObject>` will no longer be required simply to create a paragraph of flowing text.

Text Elements and Attributes

There are three text container elements in SVG: <text>, <tspan>, and <textPath>. However, both <tspan> and <textPath> must always be used *inside* a <text> element. Also described here is the <foreignObject> element, which is most commonly used to add HTML text to an SVG.

<text>

A self-contained sequence of text content to be included in the graphic, possibly including child elements with styled or positioned text.

x

The horizontal position of the anchor point or points

- A list of space- or comma-separated lengths (with units or as numbers of user units) or percentages (of the coordinate system width)

- Values are assigned to individual characters in the text content of this or child elements

- Default is a single value 0

y

The vertical position of the anchor point or points

- A list of space- or comma-separated lengths (with units or as numbers of user units) or percentages (of the coordinate system width)

- Values are assigned to individual characters in the text content of this or child elements
- Default is a single value 0

dx

The horizontal offsets to be applied to each character's position

- A list of space- or comma-separated lengths (with units or as numbers of user units) or percentages (of the coordinate system width)
- Values are assigned to individual characters in the text content of this or child elements
- Default is an empty list (no additional offsets)

dy

The vertical offsets to be applied to each character's position

- A list of space- or comma-separated lengths (with units or as numbers of user units) or percentages (of the coordinate system width)
- Values are assigned to individual characters in the text content of this or child elements
- Default is an empty list (no additional offsets)

rotate

A rotation to be applied to each character

- A list of space- or comma-separated numbers, representing angles in degrees
- Values are assigned to individual characters; however, a final value is repeated as necessary for all remaining characters within this element or its children
- Default is the single value 0

textLength

The expected or desired total offset length of this text element, including all child content

- A length (with units or as numbers of user units)

- Default is to use the `textLength` computed by the browser, without adjustment

`lengthAdjust`
The parts of the text that the browser may modify if required to match the `textLength` value

- One of the values `spacing` or `spacingAndGlyphs`
- Default `spacing`

`<tspan>`
A section of text content with distinct styles or positioning attributes. Attributes are the same as for `<text>` *except* for the following differences:

- Any values for a given character for x, y, dx, dy, or `rotate` supersede values specified for the same character on parent elements
- The defaults for x and y are empty lists: no absolute positioning is applied

`<textPath>`
A section of text that should be arranged along the outline of a path

`xlink:href`
A reference to the path that should be used to position the text

- A URL with a target fragment that matches the `id` of a `<path>` element
- Theoretically, the `<path>` could be in a different document, but this has limited support
- In XML documents (including SVG), the `xlink` prefix must be attached to the XLink namespace, *http://www.w3.org/1999/xlink*, using an `xmlns:xlink` attribute
- If not specified, or if the `<path>` cannot be located, the text content will not be drawn

startOffset
The position along the path at which to anchor the text

- A length (with units or as a number of user units) measured from the start of the path, or a percentage of the path's length
- Default 0

method
Whether the browser should align individual characters along the path, or stretch them around curves while maintaining connections between them. No effect in web browsers currently.

spacing
A hint to the browser on whether glyphs should be positioned at exact (default) distances along the path or whether optimizations can be used (auto). No effect in web browsers currently.

<foreignObject>
A container element for a block of XML content in a non-SVG namespace, which should be rendered into a specified region of the SVG.

x
Horizontal position of the corner of the foreign content area that has minimum coordinates

- A length (in user coordinates or with units) or percentage (of coordinate system width)
- Default 0

y
Vertical position of the corner of the foreign content area that has minimum coordinates

- A length (in user coordinates or with units) or percentage (of coordinate system height)
- Default 0

`width`
> The width in which to position the foreign content

- A length (in user coordinates or with units) or percentage (of the parent coordinate system width)
- Default 0, which disables rendering
- Negative values are an error

`height`
> The height in which to position the foreign content

- A length (in user coordinates or with units) or percentage (of the parent coordinate system height)
- Default 0, which disables rendering
- Negative values are an error

Text and Font Style Properties

This appendix summarizes all the text and font-related style properties that currently have an impact on SVG 1.1 text elements. Except where explicitly noted otherwise, they can all be defined either with CSS stylesheets, inline style attributes, or presentation attributes. Most properties are inherited by default; those that aren't are clearly indicated. Any property can be forced to inherit with the `inherit` keyword, or reset to the default value with `initial`.

You'll need to consult the main text or the specifications for details about the effect of each style value; this is primarily intended as a reference that you can flip to whenever you need to confirm the default for a property or the spelling of a keyword.

As multiline text is introduced for SVG 2, many other CSS properties will become relevant. In addition, new style properties introduced for CSS 3 may apply to SVG text.

`alignment-baseline`

Defines which point in each text glyph, perpendicular to the inline text layout orientation, should be aligned with the equivalent point in the parent text content.

- *Allowed values:*
  - One of the baseline keywords: `alphabetic`, `ideographic`, `hanging`, `mathematical`, `central`, `middle`, `text-before-edge`, `text-after-edge` (CSS 3 replaces the last two with `text-top` and `text-bottom`)

— auto or `baseline`

— In CSS 3: `top`, `bottom`, and `center`, which would use the total block dimensions instead of font baselines

- *Default:* in SVG 1.1, `auto` (not well implemented); in CSS 3, `baseline`
- *Not inherited by default*
- *Applies to:* text elements
- *Defined in:* SVG 1.1, CSS Inline Layout Level 3

`baseline-shift`

Defines an offset from the normal alignment-baseline that should apply for the extent of this element. Positive values raise the baseline, negative values lower it.

- *Allowed values:*

— A percentage of the line height (which defaults to match the font size for single-line SVG)

— A length with units

— One of the keywords `baseline`, `sub`, or `super` (CSS 3 removes `baseline`—use a length of 0 instead)

- *Default:* in SVG 1.1, `baseline`; in CSS 3, the length 0 (which has the same effect)
- *Applies to:* text elements
- *Defined in:* SVG 1.1, CSS Inline Layout Level 3

`direction`

Defines the direction of inline text layout.

- *Allowed values:* `ltr` (left-to-right) or `rtl` (right-to-left)
- *Default:* `ltr`
- *Applies to:* text elements
- *Defined in:* CSS2, CSS Writing Modes Level 3

`dominant-baseline`

Defines which point in each text glyph, perpendicular to the inline text layout orientation, should be aligned with the anchor point.

- *Allowed values:*
  - — One of the baseline keywords: `alphabetic`, `ideographic`, `hanging`, `mathematical`, `central`, `middle`, `text-before-edge`, `text-after-edge` (CSS 3 replaces the last two with `text-top` and `text-bottom`)
  - — `auto`, which means `alphabetic` for horizontal text and `central` for vertical text (CSS 3 clarifies that alphabetic baseline should also be used for sideways vertical text)
- *Default:* `auto`
- *Not inherited by default*
- *Applies to:* text elements
- *Defined in:* SVG 1.1, CSS Inline Layout Level 3

`font`

Shorthand property to set all the font-related properties (and reset those not specified to defaults). *Not defined as a presentation attribute; use the individual properties instead.*

- *Allowed values:*
  - — Any keywords for `font-style`, `font-variant`, and `font-weight`, followed by `font-size`, optionally followed by `line-height` separated with a / character, then finally a `font-family` list.
  - — One of the keywords `caption`, `icon`, `menu`, `message-box`, `small-caption`, or `status-bar`, which should set all font properties to match system defaults for that type of interface text.
- *Default:* As for individual properties
- *Applies to:* Text elements
- *Defined in:* CSS 2, SVG 1.1

`font-family`

Specifies a list of typeface families from which to select the font, from most to least preferred.

- *Allowed values:* A comma-separated list of the following options:
    - — Typeface names to be selected from the operating system's (quoted if they contain whitespace or special characters).
    - — Font-family names defined in an `@font-face` rule.
    - — One of the five generic font keywords: `serif`, `sans-serif`, `monospace`, `cursive`, `fantasy` (should be last value in the list, as these will always match a browser font).
- *Default:* Browser-specific
- *Applies to:* Text elements
- *Defined in:* CSS 2, SVG 1.1

`font-size`

Sets the size of text, by defining the height of a single line of text.

- *Allowed values:*
    - — A length or percentage; percentages and font-based relative units such as `em` and `ex` are calculated relative to the inherited font size.
    - — For SVG presentation attributes only, a unitless number that will be interpreted as a length in user coordinates.
    - — One of the keywords `xx-large`, `x-large`, `large`, `medium`, `small`, `x-small`, or `xx-small`.
    - — One of the keywords `larger` or `smaller`, which will adjust the inherited font size.
- *Default:* `medium`; however, be cautious about relying on default font sizes for SVG text within images because of browser bugs.
- *Applies to:* Text elements

- *Defined in:* CSS 2, SVG 1.1

`font-size-adjust`
Indicates that browsers should adjust the font size to maintain a specified ex height. The value is the expected ratio of ex to em units in the preferred font. If the font used by the browser has a different ratio, it should adjust the displayed font size in order to maintain the expected ex size; *however,* the actual values for em and ex units and other properties such as `line-height` will not change.

- *Allowed values:* A number between 0.0 and 1.0, or the keyword `none`

- *Default:* `none`

- *Applies to:* Text elements

- *Defined in:* CSS 2, SVG 1.1, CSS Fonts Level 3

`font-stretch`
Indicates which typeface from the specified family should be used, according to the width of the characters from narrow to wide.

- *Allowed values:* one of the keywords `normal`, `wider`, `narrower`, `ultra-condensed`, `extra-condensed`, `condensed`, `semi-condensed`, `semi-expanded`, `expanded`, `extra-expanded`, `ultra-expanded`

- *Default:* `normal`

- *Applies to:* text elements

- *Defined in:* CSS 2

`font-style`
Indicates whether an italic typeface from the specified family should be used.

- *Allowed values:* One of the keywords `normal`, `italic`, or `oblique`; unless a given font-family actually has both `italic` and `oblique` faces defined (highly unlikely), `italic` and `oblique` will be treated as synonyms.

- *Default:* `normal`

- *Applies to:* Text elements
- *Defined in:* CSS 2, SVG 1.1

`font-variant`
Indicates which typographical options should be used from the font.

- *Allowed values:*

  — In CSS 2/SVG 1.1: `normal` or `small-caps`

  — In CSS 3, `font-variant` becomes a shorthand for a number of properties for selecting OpenType font features

- *Default:* `normal`
- *Applies to:* text elements
- *Defined in:* CSS 2, CSS Fonts Level 3

`font-weight`
Indicates which typeface from the specified family should be used, according to the thickness of the strokes from light to heavy.

- *Allowed values:*

  — One of the absolute keywords `normal` or `bold`

  — One of the relative keywords `lighter` or `bolder` (which adjust relative to the inherited value)

  — A numeric weight, as a multiple of 100 between 100 and 900, where 400 is `normal` and 600 is `bold`

- *Default:* `normal`
- *Applies to:* text elements
- *Defined in:* CSS 2

`glyph-orientation-horizontal`
How glyphs should be aligned when the text writing mode is horizontal.

- *Allowed values:* `0`, `90`, `180`, or `270`
- *Default:* `0`

- *Applies to:* text elements with horizontal writing mode
- *Defined in:* SVG 1.1; deprecated by CSS Writing Modes Level 3 (use the `rotate` attribute instead)

`glyph-orientation-vertical`
How glyphs should be aligned when the text writing mode is vertical.

- *Allowed values:*

    — An angle value: `0`, `90`, `180`, or `270`

    — The keyword `auto`, which equates to 0 for full-width characters and 90 for other characters

- *Default:* `auto`
- *Applies to:* text elements with vertical writing mode
- *Defined in:* SVG 1.1; deprecated by CSS Writing Modes Level 3 (use `text-orientation` or the `rotate` attribute instead)

`kerning`
Whether font-specific spacing adjustments between glyphs should be applied.

- *Allowed values:*

    — `auto` to allow normal kerning

    — A length to impose arbitrary spacing; should only be used with length 0 to disable automatic kerning (use `letter-spacing` to alter spacing)

- *Default:* `auto`
- *Applies to:* text elements
- *Defined in:* SVG 1.1; deprecated and replaced by `font-kerning` in CSS Fonts Level 3, which only supports `auto` (kerning at the browser's discretion), `normal` (kerning as defined in the font), or `none` (no kerning)

`letter-spacing`
Determines whether and how much extra space should be added in between individual character glyphs. A non-zero value

disables all non-essential ligatures; results may be poor if the text contains essential ligatures.

- *Allowed values:*
  - — normal
  - — A length, with units or (for presentation attributes only) as a number of SVG user units
- *Default:* normal
- *Applies to:* text elements
- *Defined in:* CSS 2, SVG 1.1, CSS Text Level 3

text-anchor
Defines how each chunk of continuous text in the inline flow direction (horizontal or vertical) should be aligned relative to the anchor point in that axis (*x* or *y*).

- *Allowed values:* start, middle, or end
- *Default:* start
- *Applies to:* text elements
- *Defined in:* SVG 1.1

text-decoration
Sets the type of emphasis line, if any, that should be added along the length of the span of text.

- *Allowed values:*
  - — none
  - — Any combination of the keywords underline, overline, or line-through
  - — CSS 3 makes this a shorthand, and so would allow a combination of the values for text-decoration-position, text-decoration-style, and text-decoration-color (which would not have a direct effect for SVG)
- *Default:* none
- *Not inherited by default*
- *Applies to:* text elements

- *Defined in:* CSS 2, SVG 1.1, CSS Text Decoration Level 3

`text-orientation`
How characters should be oriented in vertical text; replaces `glyph-orientation-vertical`.

- *Allowed values:* One of the keywords `mixed`, `upright`, `sideways-right`, `sideways-left`, `sideways`, or `use-glyph-orientation`
- *Default:* `mixed`
- *Not yet supported as an SVG presentation attribute*
- *Applies to:* text elements
- *Defined in:* CSS Writing Modes Level 3

`unicode-bidi`
Determines whether the browser should apply the Unicode bidirectional algorithm to rearrange the character content to suit the layout direction.

- *Allowed values:*

    — `normal`, `embed`, or `bidi-override`

    — CSS 3 adds `isolate`, `isolate-override`, and `plaintext`

- *Default:* `normal`
- *Applies to:* text elements
- *Defined in:* CSS 2, CSS Writing Modes Level 3

`word-spacing`
Determines whether and how much extra space should be added to whitespace characters that serve as word breaks in the text.

- *Allowed values:*

    — `normal`

    — A length, with units or (for presentation attributes only) as a number of SVG user units

— CSS 3 adds a percentage option, where the percentage is an increase relative to the normal spacing for that white-space character

- *Default:* normal
- *Applies to:* text elements
- *Defined in:* CSS 2, SVG 1.1, CSS Text Level 3

writing-mode

Defines the layout orientation for text.

- *Allowed values:*
  — In SVG 1.1, lr, lr-tb, rl, rl-tb for horizontal text; in CSS 3, horizontal-tb
  — In SVG 1.1, tb and tb-rl for vertical text; in CSS 3, vertical-rl
  — In CSS 3, vertical-lr
- *Default:* in SVG 1.1, lr-tb; in CSS 3, horizontal-tb
- *Applies to:* text elements
- *Defined in:* SVG 1.1, CSS Writing Modes Level 3

Index

inline SVG for HTML text effects, 48, 59, 180

inline SVG style inheritance, 29, 52

lang attribute, 11

plain text content, behavior versus SVG, 23

semantic elements, versus ARIA roles, 40

simulating foreignObject, 193

styling text with CSS, 16

whitespace collapsing, 100

hyphenation, 15

I

IANA (Internet Assigned Numbers Authority), 10

ideographic baseline, 124

inline-size style property, SVG 2, 79

interactivity, 45

Internet Assigned Numbers Authority (IANA), 10

Internet Explorer/Edge browser

baseline properties support, 123, 128

bidirectional text bugs, 105

CSS transform support, 24

fallbacks for IE8, 23, 52

focus control, 45, 56

@font-face support in images, 159

font-family name matching, 156

font-size-adjust support, 31

foreignObject support, 186

inline SVG and bidirectional text, 109

inline SVG and text-decoration, 57

right-to-left text on textPath, 141

rotated text appearance with gradients and patterns, 91

start/end text-align, 104

SVG fonts support, 17

text-shadow and CSS 3 text-decoration support, 37

textLength support, 173, 179

textPath positioning bugs, 145

vertical text support, 110-111, 128

whitespace collapsing bug, 100

xml:space support, 100

K

kerning, defined, 14

kerning style property, 207

L

lang attribute, HTML, 11

:lang() CSS selector, 40

language, 2

declaring in HTML and XML/SVG, 11

script versus, 2

lengthAdjust attribute, 179, 197

letter-spacing and word-spacing style properties, 31, 83, 83, 207, 209

impact on alignment, 97

to improve spacing in textPath, 150

textLength versus, 179

ligatures, 4

character positioning, 83

stroked text and, 142

line breaks, using positioning attributes, 72

linearGradient element, 58

(see also gradients and patterns)

local() CSS function, @font-face rule, 163

M

mathematical baseline, 124

MathML, within foreignObject, 186

method attribute, textPath element, 148, 198

Microsoft Edge browser (see Internet Explorer/Edge)

middle baseline, 124

middle keyword, 93

(see also text-anchor)

monospace fonts, 152

(see also font families)

N

@namespace CSS rule, 190

focus control, 45
@font-face support in images, 159
font-size tiny in images, 24, 26
font-size-adjust support, 31
inline SVG and bidirectional text, 109
inline SVG and text-decoration, 57
inline SVG overflow, 50
mixed-case selectors not recognized, 144, 178
right-to-left text on textPath, 139, 141
rotated text appearance with gradients and patterns, 91
SVG fonts support, 17
text-shadow and CSS 3 text-decoration support, 37
textLength support, 173
textPath startOffset clipping, 140
vertical text support, 110-111, 128
WebKit-prefixed style properties, 51, 59
xml:space support, 100
-webkit-background-clip style property, 59
-webkit-text-stroke style property, 51
white-space style property, SVG 2, 101
whitespace
default behavior, 81, 100
impact on text alignment, 97-98
preserving, 100

width attribute, foreignObject element, 186, 199
WOFF (Web Open Font Format), 13, 164
(see also font files)
writing-mode style property, 110, 210
(see also vertical text)
in CSS 3, 114

X

x attribute, 22, 68, 195
(see also positioning attributes)
default text versus tspan, 68
foreignObject element, 186, 198
multiple values, 81
xlink:href attribute
gradients, 61
textPath element, 137, 197
xml:lang attribute, 11, 40
(see also language)
xml:space attribute, 100

Y

y attribute, 22, 68, 195
(see also positioning attributes)
default text versus tspan, 68
foreignObject element, 186, 198
multiple values, 81

Z

zero-width characters, 132
(see also character entitites)

About the Authors

Amelia Bellamy-Royds is a freelance writer specializing in scientific and technical communication. She is best known in web design circles for her writings about SVG. Amelia is an Invited Expert on the W3C's SVG Working Group, and is also active in the SVG Accessibility Task Force. She helps promote web standards and design through participation in online communities such as Web Platform Docs, Stack Exchange, and Codepen.

Amelia's interest in SVG stems from work in data visualization, and builds upon the programming fundamentals she learned while earning a B.Sc. in bioinformatics. From there, she moved to work in science, health, and environment policy research, and then to a master's degree in journalism. Amelia currently lives in Edmonton, Alberta. If she isn't at a computer, she's probably digging in her vegetable garden or out enjoying live music.

Kurt Cagle worked as a member of the SVG Working Group, and wrote one of the first SVG books on the market in 2004. Currently an Invited Expert with the W3C Xforms working group, Kurt is also an XML Data Architect for the Library of Congress, after having worked in that role for the US National Archives. He has been a regular contributor to O'Reilly Media since 2003, and was an online editor in 2008–2009.

Colophon

The animal on the cover of *SVG Text Layout* is a Cabot's tragopan (*Tragopan caboti*). This small, plump, ground-dwelling, and resourceful pheasant is endemic to a small, subtropical forested area of southeast China that includes the provinces of Fujian, Guangdong, Guangzi, Hunan, Jianxi, and Zhejiang.

The males are highly colorful, having heavily buff-spotted, rich reddish-brown upperparts, straw-buff underparts, and a blackish head with bare orange facial skin (including brilliant blue and red inflatable "lappet" and "horn" wattles), golden crown-sides, and orange-red neck-sides. The females, smaller than the males by a pound, are sober in their appearance, having a reddish-brown head spotted with black, and brown and gray feathers spotted with white chevrons.

Foraging by day on the ground, they roost at night in the boughs of the *Daphniphyllum macropodum*, a small tree that conveniently provides the leaves and fruit that are a dietary staple. Breeding takes place in spring, with the female clutching and incubating two to six eggs, which hatch in about 28 days. After two to three days of brooding, the chicks are able to fly. The family then leaves their nest, remaining together throughout the winter—sometimes joining another family, dwelling above the tree line in large trees near the ridge tops.

Although officially designated by the International Union for Conservation of Nature as being a "vulnerable species" due to its small population and rapid habitat conversion and fragmentation, *Tragopan caboti* has found ways to incorporate the trappings of modern infrastructure to their native habitat into their daily lives. The soft, quiet, clay roads running through a large nature reserve in Jiangxi province provides opportunities for feeding and grit collection, as well as an additional venue for their elaborate courtship rituals.

Many of the animals on O'Reilly covers are endangered; all of them are important to the world. To learn more about how you can help, go to *animals.oreilly.com*.

The cover image is by Karen Montgomery, based on a black and white engraving from *Cambridge Natural History*. The cover fonts are URW Typewriter and Guardian Sans. The text font is Adobe Minion Pro; the heading font is Adobe Myriad Condensed; and the code font is Dalton Maag's Ubuntu Mono.

Milton Keynes UK
Ingram Content Group UK Ltd.
UKHW021147010824
446294UK00012B/64

9 781491 933824